The North of the South

Mercer University Lamar Memorial Lectures No. 59

THE NORTH
OF THE SOUTH

The Natural World and
the National Imaginary in
the Literature of the Upper South

BARBARA LADD

THE UNIVERSITY OF GEORGIA PRESS   Athens

© 2022 by the University of Georgia Press
Athens, Georgia 30602
www.ugapress.org
All rights reserved

Set in 10/14 Sabon by Rebecca A. Norton

Most University of Georgia Press titles are
available from popular e-book vendors.

Printed digitally

Library of Congress Cataloging-in-Publication Data
Names: Ladd, Barbara, author.
Title: The north of the South :
the natural world and the national imaginary
in the literature of the upper South / Barbara Ladd.
Description: Athens : The University of Georgia Press, 2022. |
Series: Mercer University Lamar memorial lectures; 59 |
Includes bibliographical references and index.
Identifiers: LCCN 2022010892 | ISBN 9780820362519 (hardback) |
ISBN 9780820362526 (paperback) | ISBN 9780820362533 (ebook)
Subjects: LCSH: American literature—Southern authors—
History and criticism. | Nature in literature. | Southern States—
In literature. | Southern States—Intellectual life.
Classification: LCC PS261 .L336 2022 |
DDC 810.9/975—dc23/eng/20220418
LC record available at https://lccn.loc.gov/2022010892

Contents

꙲

Acknowledgments

꧁꧂

The subjects I take up in this book and in the talks from which it is derived have been uppermost in my mind for years, and I would like to extend my sincere thanks to Mercer University and to the Lamar Memorial Lectures Committee for their invitation to speak. Had I not received Doug Thompson's call, I doubt the project would have taken the direction it has taken, and I doubt that a longer book on these subjects would be in the works.

My visit to Mercer was both an honor and a pleasure, from beginning to end, and I want to extend my sincere thanks to David Davis, Sarah Gardner, and Andrew Silver, as well as to Doug, for making my visit such a pleasant one. Bobbie Shipley made sure that everything was in order and running smoothly, no simple matter when hosting a university visitor, as I well know; my thanks to her as well. And thanks also to Bethany Snead, Jon Davies, and others at the University of Georgia Press, as well as Arthur Johnson, for much expert assistance.

The teachers, scholars, and writers I reference in this book, and many whom I have not referenced, have given me more over the years than I can properly thank them for.

The North of the South

Introduction

꙲

Over the past generation the Deep South has become the primary site and the plantation the predominant referent in southern literary studies, developments that have followed academic interest, first in postcolonial studies and more recently in globalization studies and its "Global South" terrain. In this book, I'd like to divert some attention northward, to the Upper South, to "the North of the South."[1]

To be sure, the work that has come out of what we might call Global American South studies continues to be important and calls our attention to the many ways in which the cultures of the southern United States are tied to cultures to the south of the American South—the Caribbean, Africa, and Central and South America have been of most interest to students of the U.S. South. My first book, *Nationalism and the Color Line in George W. Cable, Mark Twain, and William Faulkner* (published what seems like a lifetime ago, in 1996), helped to inaugurate the Caribbean turn in southern studies. Since that time, more (and better) work has appeared, and I remain interested in the revelations of Global American South studies.

Lately, however, I have become more interested in the Upper South, in the British rather than the French and Spanish colonies, and in the quite different cultures and literatures we find coming out of Virginia, Maryland, Delaware, North Carolina, Tennessee, and Kentucky. As historians like Jack P. Greene have reminded us, plantations in the Upper South were initially established by people who proposed to settle in the New World and brought their families (unlike many of those in the French and Spanish territories of what is now the Deep South and in the Global South more broadly). The descendants of those settlers became central figures in the American Revolution, the first New World war of independence.

Upper South plantations were different in other ways. They shared more of the land with farms and towns. They were sometimes smaller and, importantly, less stable over time—plantations in the Upper South began to fail by the early nineteenth century, only a generation after the American Revolution. In part, this had to do with the fact that tobacco production exhausted the soil so quickly; and although the Sugar Revolution made fortunes for planters in the Deep South and the Caribbean, the Upper South was hardly suitable for sugar agriculture, or even for cotton production on a large scale. As a result, some planters sent their sons into lands newly acquired from France in the Deep South to recoup, while others migrated across the Appalachians into Tennessee and Kentucky, and farther still, into the Midwest.

In the Upper South we find a more, or at least differently, diverse population as well. There was a large population of free persons of color, for example, some of whom descended from laborers brought from Africa in the decades before slavery began to be codified for persons of African descent in the middle of the seventeenth century. The post-contact history of Native American cultures in the Upper South more closely resembles the history of such cultures in New England and the Mid-Atlantic—in short, Native Americans were pushed westward earlier in the Upper South than in the Deep South. And proximity to the Mid-Atlantic made some cities, such as Richmond and Baltimore, more like Philadelphia and New York than like New Orleans.

In fact, the boundary between the Upper South and the Mid-Atlantic has always been uncertain, as has the boundary between the Upper South and the Midwest (although the fluidity of the latter is more often recognized). As one historian reminds us, the very category of "middle colonies" and "middle states" was late to develop, and a case can be made that what we today think of as the Mid-Atlantic (New York, Pennsylvania, Delaware, New Jersey, Maryland) was actually two regions during the colonial period and in the Early Republic, with New York and New Jersey being more closely aligned, culturally and economically, with New England, and Pennsylvania, Maryland, and Delaware more closely aligned with Virginia. Moreover, Virginia itself has at times been classified as a "middle state" (Gough 397–401).

None of this is to say that Virginia, Delaware, and Maryland were not part of the plantation complex. They were, as were parts of New Jersey, New York, and Massachusetts. However, turning our attention to the Upper South recasts southern culture vis-à-vis the American project, the Global South, and the Global North in ways that can illuminate the role not only of the plantation but of life beyond the plantation proper in the national project and in the literary imaginations of southerners in and beyond the North of the South. It calls into question the rigid mapping of regions in American literary and cultural studies and challenges some of the fixed ideas we still have about American regional differences.

In this study, I foreground the natural world and the role it played in the national imaginary of Upper South writers from Thomas Jefferson to Edgar Allan Poe, Elizabeth Madox Roberts, and Toni Morrison (the last of whom I include as a writer of the Upper South for reasons I explain below). The natural world of the Chesapeake Bay and Albemarle cultural hearths—a world that plays a central role in the work of all these writers—is distinctive in a number of ways. Importantly, it was associated with the nationalist agenda earlier than would be the natural world of the Deep South— much of which was acquired long after the American Revolution. Jefferson's *Notes on the State of Virginia*, for example, appeared in 1785, well before the Louisiana Purchase and Anglo-American movement into the former Louisiana Territory.

To these ends, the first two chapters focus on the world of Edgar Allan Poe, who was more of a naturalist than most people realize. I read some of Poe's work as a melancholy response to the national and environmental imagination of that other famous Virginia naturalist, Thomas Jefferson. In this move, I hope to suggest the difference ecoregionalism might make both for our understanding of southern literature and literary history and for our understanding of the American cultural project. In the final chapter, I look northward and westward from Richmond and the Blue Ridge into and beyond the Appalachians to explore the worlds of Elizabeth Madox Roberts, Cormac McCarthy (very briefly), and Toni Morrison—all of whom (along with Poe) recast the narrative of nation building in a melancholy tenor, as stories of loss and forgetting, and all of whom are remarkable nature writers.

CHAPTER ONE

Southern Literary Studies

Then and Now

It is a curious process, that by which an explanation self-evident to one generation ceases to hold meaning for the next.
— MICHAEL O'BRIEN, "A HETERODOX NOTE
ON THE SOUTHERN RENAISSANCE"

Louis D. Rubin Jr. often told the story of trying to find a director for his dissertation at Johns Hopkins University. He approached "an American literature scholar of some reputation, who liked very much to think of himself as a Southern gentleman," and proposed a dissertation on Thomas Wolfe "as a Southern writer." The scholar responded that Thomas Wolfe wasn't a southern writer, that he belonged "in spirit . . . among the Midwestern writers." Why? Because Wolfe was not a "gentleman," and according to received wisdom, southern literature, like the South itself, was defined by its "aristocratic ideal" ("Thomas Wolfe"). This was in the early 1950s. Rubin went on to find a director for his dissertation and, over the next few years, began to lay the foundations for an institutionalization of southern literary studies, drawing on the work of the Southern Renaissance writers and the academics who studied them (Cleanth Brooks, Robert Penn Warren, and others). These were the years of the GI Bill and the proliferation of new programs of study in American colleges and universities. It was the era of the United States' supremacy on the world stage, of the ascendancy of "the greatest generation," of the baby boom and the civil rights movement, and of economic expansion and prosperity throughout the United

States, including the South, which, fewer than twenty years before, Franklin D. Roosevelt had deemed "the nation's number 1 economic problem." The southern middle class was growing.

"Southern studies" became an academic field in these years. Mercer University's Lamar Memorial Lectures in Southern History and Culture began in 1957, when Spencer B. King Jr. established the Center for Southern Studies. The Institute for Southern Studies was established in Durham in 1970, and the Center for the Study of Southern Culture was founded at the University of Mississippi in 1975. By 1990, when I finished my degree at the University of North Carolina at Chapel Hill, southern literature was more than a field of study—it had become an industry, a regional literature that transcended regionalism. Ironically, the Center for the Study of the American South at UNC–Chapel Hill, Rubin's home institution, was not established until 1992. And Vanderbilt University has never had a center for southern studies—the Robert Penn Warren Center is devoted to the humanities and interdisciplinary work more generally.

By the 1960s, southern literary study seemed to be moving beyond any consensus that an "aristocratic ideal" defined the South or its literature, at least in some circles. When C. Hugh Holman, in *Three Modes of Modern Southern Fiction: Ellen Glasgow, William Faulkner, Thomas Wolfe* (delivered as part of the Lamar Lectures in 1966), divided the literary South into three subregions—the Tidewater and Low Country South, the Gulf Coast or Deep South, and the Piedmont and Mountain South, distinguished by "race, geography, climate, and religion" (xii)—he not only challenged the idea of a monolithic South but also paved the way for Rubin, only a few years later, to add "class" to Holman's list of features differentiating the southern subregions. In "Southern Literature: A Piedmont Art," Rubin argued that the "really major southern writers" were "raised above the fall line" (4). What he meant was that they were mostly middle class. For Rubin, the

Tidewater and Low Country South was synonymous with the "aristocratic ideal," and the Piedmont and Mountain South was identified with the middle classes.

In making his claim for the preeminence of the southern middle classes, as authors and as subjects, in literature, Rubin wrote the South—culturally and ideologically—back into a more broadly "American" myth, claiming for the South a dominant literary culture that was, in its own way, not so far outside the American mainstream. He described a South that was itself a modern and capitalist project, even in its embrace of slavery in the nineteenth century, its "aristocratic ideal" more a matter of style and pretense than anything else. But around the same time, Eugene Genovese presented a different perspective in *The World the Slaveholders Made*, arguing that the South was indeed an anachronistic outpost of a precapitalist and paternalistic culture. Then in 1988, Elizabeth Fox-Genovese published *Within the Plantation Household: Black and White Women of the Old South*; as its title indicates, her study, like her husband's work, focused on southern paternalism and on the plantation as the defining institution of the South. Rubin's perspective notwithstanding, the antebellum South and the long arm of the plantation, with its "aristocratic ideal," would not easily be displaced.

Then New Southern Studies appeared. Exactly what New Southern Studies was remains up for debate. Much of the rhetoric surrounding its initial appearance focused on what Scott Romine and Jennifer Rae Greeson, in *Keywords for Southern Studies*, identify as "generational affinities" (1), and it never had much in the way of ideological or methodological tone. New Southern Studies was fundamentally opportunistic. Even the moment at which it is said to have originated floats between the mid-1990s and the early 2000s, depending on who is speaking and on who or what is being claimed as originary for any particular purpose.

Ultimately, however, New Southern Studies was capacious enough to be useful for a range of work, both traditional and new, from close readings of canonical literature to political, cultural, identitarian, or nonidentitarian positionings of various kinds. This was its strength, enabling a firm breaking away from a mid-twentieth-century, Cold War–era model of southern literary studies. When Romine and Greeson note that the question is no longer "What is southern studies studying?" but "What does southern studies *do*?" (3), the credit belongs largely to New Southern Studies.

At this point, New Southern Studies has passed into history, joining other movements and moments in the rich literary traditions from which present work emerges. Today, thanks to Holman, Rubin, New Southern Studies, other movements, and many other people, southern studies operates on a very different set of assumptions than it did in the past. In the first place, "The South," the monolith, has been replaced not only with what Holman termed "subregions" but with what Scott Romine calls "microSouths" (*The Real South* 15). The three Souths of the midcentury (Tidewater and Low Country, Piedmont and Mountain, and Deep) have multiplied as the territorial imaginaries of southern literature and literary histories have proliferated: coastal Souths, the Rural South, the Black Belt, Urban Souths, Border Souths, Virtual and "Reel" Souths, the American South and the U.S. South (different from each other), all of the above but without the capital "S"—and, everywhere you look, the Global South, or, more accurately, the "Global American South."

I won't try to further characterize the present moment in southern studies—always a risky undertaking—except to say that the major legacy of New Southern Studies, the legacy with the greatest power to define and mobilize, is Global American South studies. When Coleman Hutchison, defining New Southern Studies, pointed to its interest in a "constell[ation]" of "southern localities in relation to a number of non- or extra-national cultural configurations," he specified "the global South, the native or indigenous South, and Greater Mexico" (694); in so doing, he gestured to something important if usually unstated: not only did New Southern Studies arise in the wake of independence movements in former colonies and resistance movements in feudal and authoritarian cultures, but it was animated by the idea of the American South itself as colonized space, as "the nation's region" (Duck) or "our South" (Greeson). Global American South studies tends of course to be considerably less interested in the fact that the American/U.S. South is at least as much a part of the Global North.

At any rate, studies of the microSouths, for all the different class positions we find across them, have not yet generated a new paradigm for southern studies. Global American South studies finds its most powerful explanatory structure in "The Plantation," or what Amy Clukey and Jeremy Wells have identified as the "plantation imaginary" (4), and the subregion of most significance (or at least of most interest) is the Deep South, where ties to the Global South are easier to discern (not that they aren't present elsewhere). Interest in the middle classes and in the Piedmont and Upper South has declined with the ascent of Global American South studies in the paradigm shifts associated initially with postcolonial theories of development and later with Global South emphases on power relations that have redirected attention to the relations between elites (planters, their agents, and their descendants in modern corporate culture) and subordinates (enslaved persons, workers, immigrants—i.e., underclasses).

No one would deny the importance of this work. The plantation is a very significant site for explorations of southern literature and literary history, and one with global relevance, but its narratives—of race, class, ecology—can be oversimplified and static. Ultimately the foregrounding of the plantation as the defining institution of the South, with its agricultural monoculture, its stifling of the development of a middle class, its rural world of planters and servile labor (both Black and poor white), its "aristocratic ideal" if you will, and its contemporary manifestation in corporate and State power—as significant as all that is, especially now, with the middle class disappearing across the country and white nationalism once again on the rise—is only part of the story. Permitting that story to dominate the field is to silence many of the voices and traditions within the South that would make alternatives to that new monolith much easier to imagine.

As for the question of the environment and the prospects of environmentalisms in southern literary history: when Holman included geography and climate in his list of features that define the South, "eco" was not in the vocabulary of literary scholars, and geography and climate were relevant only as background for economic and social life. The idea, expressed most succinctly by Benedetto Croce, was that we do not "understand ourselves best as part of the natural world" (D. Roberts 59). Over the past generation, however, in response to environmental crisis, a new environmentally based criticism has appeared in the work of a growing number of scholars to argue that perhaps we DO understand ourselves best as part of the natural world.

Today, the natural world has become central to literary and cultural studies, and we are seeing a redefinition of the idea of "place." Charles Reagan Wilson writes in *The New Encyclopedia of Southern Culture* that place "implies an organic society" (253). I suspect many of us who came of age in the mid-twentieth century and afterward in the South do not feel that we belong, or that we ever belonged, to an organic society, at least not in the sense Wilson means—the sense in which everyone not only knows his or her place but finds the future there. I, an urban southerner growing up during the civil rights and women's movements, found talk about "place" ("know your place," "don't get above your raisin'," "remember who you are") to be a threatening remnant of the mysterious repressions of the world in which my parents and grandparents grew up.

For a time in the theory-heavy 1990s, students of literature and culture gravitated to the word "space," which perhaps sounds more . . . spacious, as in "Give me my space," useful for liberatory discourses. People sometimes use the terms "place" and "space" interchangeably. But Edward Casey, a historian of philosophy whom I admire and the author of *The Fate of Place*, has very usefully distinguished between "space"—which can be best represented on a grid in which "spaces" are "sites" and are interchangeable, a quantitative concept (how much, how large, etc.)—and "place," which cannot be so easily represented on a grid and is a qualitative concept associated with memory and the body. This is the difference between a geometric site, with dimensions that are "metrically determined" and isotropic, and a qualitative concept, memory being dependent on the body and the body being anisotropic. That we are embodied means that we understand up, down, right, left, forward, backward, now, then—we are not "lost in space."

But, as Casey demonstrates, modernity increasingly substituted "space" for "place" from the Renaissance forward. Modernity's preference for "space" over "place," we might say, is one product of a "normalizing"/"standardizing" agenda: is it normal or not, we ask, and can we get a replacement part if it breaks? If it isn't "normal," if it isn't "standardized," it is either extraordinarily valuable or useless, or both—and this applies as much to natural and human resources as to aesthetic objects.

So something *is* lost in that substitution, something increasingly important. In this book, I want to suggest some ways to recover, for southern literary history, a viable idea of place in the way that Michael Kowalewski understands it. As he observed a number of years ago, new "literary mappings of American places" are based on "metaphors of depth, resonance, root systems, habitats, and interconnectedness—factors that together put places into motion, making them move within their own history, both human and nonhuman" (182).[1]

To "put places into motion," to permit them to "move within their own history, both human and nonhuman," I explore the traces of what I have called the "crossroads local" ("Local Places" 111) in a selection of literary texts. These are sites of encounter, exchange, and adaptation across time— places where writing itself is resistant to the normalizing/standardizing agenda of modernity, sometimes through the production of the grotesque, of the peculiarity within; of whatever is deviant, anachronistic, or idiosyncratic within any standardizing agenda; of the monstrous birth or the strange and unexpected irruption. I am interested in the heterogeneous, the unassimilated and unacculturated, whether it manifests itself in the work of Edgar Allan Poe (the greatest "odd man out" of southern and American literary history); or in that of the neglected Elizabeth Madox Roberts; or in the work of Toni Morrison, whose vision of American origins and prospects runs powerfully against the grain of our most celebratory narratives. In all of this, I hope to bring the natural world more fully into the conversation, to question received cartographies and to argue that the regionalizations institutionalized in American literary histories constitute an imagined geography that is no longer viable (if it ever was) and precludes the development of a new and better understanding of ourselves as creations of a natural world that not only surrounds but also inhabits us.

Looking ahead to the next chapter and to Poe, I'd like to sketch out the worlds he would have known—the natural world around him in "the North of the South" and the social one.

First, the Chesapeake Bay and the Tidewater: this is a coastal plain that extends from northeastern North Carolina to Maryland and westward to Richmond, where the falls of the James River mark the Fall Line that Holman found so significant and that separates the higher land of hard rocks leading westward to the Appalachians from the softer soil to the east, a transitional area distinguished by falling water (rapids, cataracts, etc.). Richmond is on the Fall Line. In the United

States, the Fall Line separates the Atlantic Coastal Plain from the Piedmont, beginning in New Jersey. In the South it runs through Baltimore to Richmond, Raleigh, and Columbia, down to Milledgeville and Macon, and over to Huntsville, Alabama. To the east and south of the Fall Line is the Tidewater and Low Country South, and above it is the Piedmont and Mountain South.

Wetlands and swamps are prominent features throughout the Tidewater area. In the Chesapeake and Albemarle Tidewater, the Great Dismal Swamp is a major landmark that extends from just south of Norfolk in southeastern Virginia to just north of Elizabeth City, North Carolina.

The English first settled in the region of the Tidewater in the early seventeenth century. It is, among other things, a place where the South meets the Mid-Atlantic—where the South meets the North—and of course there is no actual dividing line between North and South. What there is instead is a system of rivers, trails, roads, and highways that connects, for example, Southampton, Virginia, to Richmond to Washington, DC, to Baltimore to Philadelphia and New York— with the exception of Southampton and Washington, these are cities in which Poe lived.

There are certain singular features of the land here. Roy Sawyer, in *America's Wetland*, points out that the Albemarle tidewater region of coastal North Carolina and Virginia is "one of the largest freshwater wetlands in the nation." This Albemarle region begins in Suffolk, Virginia, and ends in the White Oak River area of Carteret County in North Carolina. The Albemarle Peninsula is its center, but it also includes the Tar-Neuse river basin. "Like nowhere else on earth," Sawyer writes, "the Albemarle region juts abruptly into the Atlantic Ocean, deflecting the warm Gulf Stream away from the mainland toward Europe," which means that it "is the last, northernmost point on the American continent warmed by the Gulf Stream" (4). The "Great Alligator Swamp" on the Albemarle Peninsula is "the northernmost home of the American alligator" (4). Here you can sometimes find animals from a more northerly climate and animals from warmer climates in the same habitat (14–15). When the first European explorers landed, there were black bears (still there as a relict population); red wolves (recently reintroduced); bison (4–5); and the Carolina dog (30), the only feral dog native to North America. Edgar Allan Poe would have seen passenger pigeons and the Carolina parakeet, both now extinct. As for flora, there were and still are huge trees, some of them more than sixteen hundred years old, "the oldest living things east of the Rocky Mountains" (5). The region is more susceptible to hurricanes than the rest of the United States—"a veritable hurricane alley" (5)—and is the home of the mysterious Lake Drummond, named for a North Carolina governor and located at the center of the Great Dismal Swamp.

It is always surprising that so few people have heard of the Great Dismal Swamp, which is one of the most storied swamps in American culture. Native American legends abound—the legend of the Deer Tree, for example, a bald cypress deep in the swamp; according to this legend, a deer, hunted, changed itself into a tree for protection. We can discern a trace of this legend in North Carolina writer Charles Chesnutt's story "Po' Sandy," in which the enslaved Sandy is changed into a tree for his protection and is eventually hewn down for the lumber to build a schoolhouse. The sawing produces a scream that terrifies the workers. The sentience of vegetable life is a theme that Edgar Allan Poe had explored almost fifty years before—and it's something I will take up in the next chapter.

The hero of Martin Delany's novel *Blake* finds a remnant of Africa in the old maroons he encounters in the Great Dismal Swamp; these self-emancipated fugitives from slavery found refuge in the swamp's depths, safe from slave hunters, as did other fugitives from the laws or conventions of the time and place. Harriet Beecher Stowe writes about the swamp and marronage in *Dred: A Tale of the Great Dismal Swamp*; Harriet Jacobs may have passed through on her way to freedom; Moses Grandy's enslavement narrative tells of his time as a "captain" bringing cedar shingles out of the swamp; nineteenth-century landscape artists drew and painted the swamp; and in "Philosophy of Furniture," Edgar Allan Poe advises that tasteful homes have a painting "of an imaginative cast" like that of John Gadsby Chapman's *The Lake of the Dismal Swamp* (502). The Irish poet Thomas Moore visited Norfolk and wrote a ballad while there about the spirit of an Indian maiden and her lover who can be seen paddling their canoe at midnight on Lake Drummond. In 1894 Robert Frost went there with the intention to commit suicide after a failed love affair. Daniel Sayers, an archaeologist at American University in Washington, and his students are excavating in the swamp and have found evidence of human settlement from the beginnings of slavery in the area until the end of the Civil War.

Scientists still don't understand how the Dismal Swamp was formed, or the reasons for some of its surprising features. Unlike in most swamps, the streams flow out rather than in toward the swamp; the swamp is not lower but *higher* in elevation than the surrounding area. It is filled with bogs of evergreens, loblolly pines, cypress, brier thickets—a mixed forest of red maple, pond pine, and Atlantic white cedar. Lake Drummond is almost black to look at, but take some of the water in your hands and you'll find that it is tea colored and drinkable. One nineteenth-century writer, Léo Lesquereux, compares Lake Drummond and the swamp to raised bogs in Europe. The lake itself is young, likely only about three thousand years old, although the swamp could be as much as eighty thousand years old. George Washington sought to drain it to make it arable—but also (if truth be told) probably to rehabilitate it, to bring it under the control of the conservative Tidewater culture from which he himself came. It is a wild place. Efforts to drain it have been partly successful, and some of the farmland around its borders was reclaimed from its wetlands.

Its impenetrability, its association with outlaws, its mysteries, its unfamiliar animals and unusual plants, its depths and darkness—these features offer a resonant and suggestive contrast with the very English ideal of order we associate with European settlement in the Tidewater, and they provide a powerful metaphor with which writers and artists have conjured.

Richmond, only about sixty miles from the Great Dismal Swamp, was laid out in 1737 at the Falls of the James River, into which the freshwater of the Albemarle ecosystem flows, and in the vicinity of the "Great Indian Warpath" at the site of Powhatan's chiefdom. With respect to its social environment, Richmond was diverse. Free persons of color represented about 10 percent of Richmond's population in 1820, with a more or less equal number of women and men; such a balance was not always the case in urban enslavement sites because of the population of domestic servants, who were mostly women, but Richmond's major industries—tobacco, iron, and coal—ensured a larger than usual population of Black men. During Poe's time, white Richmond remained very English, and Richmond was then, as it is now, an "American city in a Southern place," as Gregg Kimball puts it.[2]

Baltimore, not very far from Richmond and also northward facing (and where Poe's father was from), was in the antebellum years the home of the largest population of free Blacks in the nation (McNeil). Undoubtedly this would be a surprise to most Americans today, for whom freedom in the antebellum United States lay north, which it definitely did for fugitives. But because this was the Upper South, settled well before slavery became codified into the institution we are most familiar with, there was a nascent population of free persons of color as early as the seventeenth century—and because of the coastal location and the prevalence of swamps and other features of the natural environment during the contact and colonial periods, movement (whether by escape or self-emancipation through marronage) was more likely than in some other locations. Fugitives were notoriously hard to trace.

To venture a bit further back in time: the early modern period, which begins in the fifteenth century and, for some, extends until 1800 (including the period in which John Allan, who would become Poe's foster father, arrived in Richmond), was certainly still viable as a residual culture in the 1810s, when Poe was growing up. In a 2007 study Jack P. Greene points out that there was "extraordinary" cultural diversity in the southeastern part of North America in the early modern period. In the sixteenth and seventeenth centuries, the Spanish, the French, and the English established different kinds of colonial projects in the New World. Unlike the French and the Spanish, though, the English came to Maryland, Virginia, and North and South Carolina, and later to Georgia, "with settlement as their principal objective." By the time of the American Revolution, English settlers "occupied most of the area up to the Appalachian Mountains" and were already "spilling across those mountains" ("Early Modern" 528). There was nothing comparable in French and Spanish plantation colonies in what is now the Deep South.

Greene also points out that the settlements in the Chesapeake, which included some of the northeastern parts of North Carolina, "differed radically from those to the south." Among the differences were "a mixed agricultural economy," with tobacco as the staple crop, not the expected plantation monoculture; and the use of indentured servants through the seventeenth century, with enslaved Africans displacing indentured servants only in the first few decades of the eighteenth century—a reality that helped lay the foundations for the relatively large population of free persons of color in the region. And importantly, plantations employing thirty or more enslaved persons took up less than one-fifth of the land devoted to tobacco. In other words, plantations were comparatively small and coexisted with small farms, with yeoman farms dominating and yeoman farmers participating in what Greene calls a "consensual" civic culture quite different from the imperial cultures of those French and Spanish colonies where settlement was not so much on the agenda ("Early Modern" 529)—and I'll reiterate here that it is somewhat problematic that the plantation models most often used today in Global American South studies are taken from the French and Spanish colonies in the Caribbean and in the former Louisiana Territory.

Greene goes on to point out that "ambivalence about slavery" and sympathy with the rhetoric of abolition coming from Europe "made some Marylanders and Virginians think of their states as *central* states that more closely resembled Pennsylvania, New Jersey, and New York" than the states to the south (530). In other words, they were northward facing. He writes:

> Beginning in the 1730s, Tidewater immigrants carried [this] Chesapeake culture, with its focus on a mixture of tobacco, corn, and grain production using slave labor distributed among a few large plantations and a much larger number of small producers, west into the Piedmont and across the Blue Ridge mountains. There they joined an even larger stream of immigrants pushing south from Pennsylvania, at once absorbing those immigrants into the broad outlines of Chesapeake culture and adapting that culture to the interests and inclinations of the newcomers. Together, these two streams of immigrants negotiated a new cultural hearth [a sphere of influence], the attributes of which a subsequent generation carried west across the Appalachians into Kentucky and south into the backcountries of the Carolinas and Georgia.

Greene concludes that "they never created a homogeneous regional southern culture." Instead, "the emerging South turned out to be at least as heterogeneous as any other area of the new United States [as] it slowly took shape in the decades after 1820" ("Early Modern" 537–38).

Here Greene sketches the trajectory of this book—from Chesapeake/Tidewater and swamp into the Piedmont and across the mountains toward the Midwest, in the North of the South, where economies, politics, and kinship tied the region to the Mid-Atlantic.

If many Americans today would be surprised to learn that the Upper South was home to a large population of free persons of color in the years before the Civil War, I suspect that most also remain in the grip of another misapprehension—that the mid-nineteenth-century white population in the United States was fully nationalized. It was not. The United States at that time was a country of immigrants, most of them from the British Isles and Western Europe, with the major ports of entry being New York, Boston, Philadelphia, and Baltimore. (These were, along with Richmond, Edgar Allan Poe's cities.) Immigration into Baltimore was significant enough that anti-Catholic riots began there in the 1830s, and by the mid-nineteenth century Baltimore was second only to New York as a U.S. port of entry. Poe lived off and on in New York in the 1830s and 1840s, when its population was almost 50 percent immigrant.

In this context, Poe's infamous deficiency in literary nationalist feeling doesn't seem as surprising as American literary history, with its focus on the development of national literary traditions, might make it seem. Our notion of our "Americanness" or our "southernness" as something that goes back to the Revolutionary era and the years of the Early Republic is of course the product of nationalist retrospective mythmaking, with its distinctive privileging of certain forms of forgetting. Ernest Renan very famously said that the "essence of a nation is, that all the individuals must have many things in common, and also that all must have forgotten many things. No French citizen knows whether he is Burgundian [. . .] or Visigoth. Every French citizen must have forgotten St. Bartholomew's night and the massacres in the southern provinces in the thirteenth century" (925). It is arguable whether white Americans in the mid-nineteenth century had forgotten their countries of origin. Immigration was ongoing. Many white

Americans were first- or second-generation immigrants. And the massacres in our "southern provinces" were not six centuries in the past but looming on the horizon.

In short, Poe was brought up not only in interesting times (a period of cultural transition from colonial to national, from early modern to modern) but in an interesting place, a place of transitions both natural and cultural—Tidewater and Chesapeake to the east, the Dismal Swamp to the southeast, the Piedmont and Blue Ridge to the west. All had an impact on him. In the next chapter I'm going to look at Poe as a "North of the South" writer, and in the final chapter I'll explore some twentieth- and twenty-first-century writing dealing with lands across the mountains, with Kentucky, and finally, with a place even farther north, which is also south.

Edgar Allan Poe

In and Out of Richmond

Richmond is my home, and a letter directed to that city will
always reach me, in whatever part of the world I may be.

— POE TO GEORGE WASHINGTON POE,

JULY 14, 1839

As I mentioned in chapter 1, Richmond was laid out in 1737.
It was a port city, open to the world, and as it grew, one
could see ships from English and European ports as well as
vessels from other American ports. Canals went eastward to
the Chesapeake Bay and westward toward the mountains
and the Cumberland Gap and toward the Ohio River. From
the beginning Richmond was a city of merchants. It served
the farms and plantations surrounding it, but it was urban,
a center for business and exchange. The city had close ties
with Great Britain through "kinship and commerce" (Bondurant 48). Betsy Ambler, daughter of Richard Ambler (and
elder sister to Mary, who would marry future chief justice
John Marshall), arrived in Richmond in 1780 and wrote that
"[w]ith the exception of two or three families this little town
is made up of Scotch factors, who inhabit small tenements
scattered here and there from the river to the hill" (qtd. in
Mattison 41).

A few years later, John Allan arrived from the Scottish
town of Dundonald and began business as a sot-weed factor,
or tobacco merchant, and he subsequently did very well in
partnership with Charles Ellis. In 1811 Allan became foster
father to a three-year-old orphan, Edgar Poe, whose mother,
the actress Elizabeth Arnold Poe, had died of tuberculosis

while in Richmond with the Placide and Green Company, a traveling theater group. Elizabeth Arnold Poe had been one of the most popular actresses on the East Coast, and Edgar had traveled with her during the first three years of his life. Edgar's father, David Poe Jr. of Baltimore, had also been an actor in the troupe (though a less talented one) but had disappeared by the time of Elizabeth's death, possibly already dead himself.

Poe would be raised in Richmond, on the Fall Line between Tidewater and Piedmont, by the sot-weed factor John Allan. The "Allan" in Poe's name was taken from John Allan, who promised to adopt Edgar but never did, a fact that left Poe with feelings of insecurity. These feelings extended beyond just Poe's emotional state, however: eventually John Allan inherited wealth and a plantation, which Edgar thought might benefit him. It didn't—after the death of Frances Allan, John's first wife and a woman Poe was extremely close to, Allan married again and fathered a child. Poe was left without the expected plantation inheritance.

As a child, before and after his time in England and Scotland between 1815 and 1820, Poe lived close to the James River, with its ships and sailors and commerce; his foster father's offices during Poe's early years were down by the docks. This was not in any sense plantation life, although as a tobacco factor Allan worked closely with planters. Henry Cogswell Knight described "the atmosphere" of Richmond at that time as "impregned with the dense murky effluvia of coal-smoke, which begrimes the pores of the skin, and affects respiration" (qtd. in Bondurant 7). Poe certainly knew the source of that "dense murky effluvia": the Heth coal mines, only a few miles outside Richmond, with their black ledges and outcroppings.

He also knew the falls and rapids of the James River. John F. D. Smyth, a British traveler, wrote in 1783 that the "cataracts" around the nascent town were its predominant feature, with their "prodigious noise and roaring" (13). In 1824 or

1825, around the age of fifteen, Poe famously swam six miles up the James (Thomas and Jackson 59, 60). He traveled to the Blue Ridge Mountains with his foster parents. He visited the mineral springs of Virginia with his foster mother on at least one occasion. During his time at the University of Virginia in Charlottesville, he was known for his long walks in the Ragged Mountains. Poe knew the Great Dismal Swamp—he was stationed on Sullivan's Island in South Carolina in 1827 for a little over a year, and it is likely that he traversed the edges of the swamp while traveling between Sullivan's Island and Richmond; he also wrote about the swamp (more about that later). Following his time in England and Scotland as a child, he never again traveled abroad. The world of the Upper South was the world with which he was most familiar, with its dark effluvia, its heights and depths, its lowlands and foothills, the mountains in the distance—and its tremendous storms.

Poe's part of the world was shaped by storms. The British burning of Washington in August 1814 was accompanied by a major storm. Poe would have been in Richmond during the great Long Island Hurricane of September 1821 and, a year later, in September 1822, during the "tropical deluge" that accompanied a major hurricane and caused flooding in the vicinity of the James River. On the Long Island Hurricane, the *Norfolk Herald* wrote:

> From half past 11 till half past 12, so great was the fury of the elements, that they seemed to threaten a general demolition of everything within their reach. During that period the scene was truly awful. The deafening roar of the storm, with the mingled crashing of windows and falling of chimneys [*sic*]— the rapid rise of the tide, threatening to inundate the town— the continuous cataracts of rain sweeping impetuously along, darkening the expanse of vision, and apparently confounding the "heaven, earth, and sea" in a general chaos; together with now and then a glimpse, caught through the gloom, of shipping, forced from their moorings and driven with rapidity, as

the mind might well conjecture in such a circumstance, to inevitable destruction. (83)

I am reminded by this description of the "confounding of 'heaven, earth, and sea' in a general chaos" and the "shipping [. . .] driven [. . .] to inevitable destruction" that we find in Poe's "A Descent into the Maelström," though that tale is set in Norway. And although Poe sets the gloom and high tides of "MS. Found in a Bottle" in the Dutch East Indies, he certainly would have known such sights from experiences come by way of the North American side of the Atlantic.

The subject of Poe's relationship to place has been debated for decades. Many have agreed with T. S. Eliot that "there can be few authors of such eminence who have drawn so little from their own roots, who have been so isolated from any surroundings" (329). But others have looked at Poe differently. Harry Levin, Jay Hubbell, Marshall McLuhan, Lewis P. Simpson, and Louis D. Rubin Jr. see in Poe a particularly southern subjectivity, especially as it is manifested in white anxiety about slavery and race and a fear of uprising by enslaved persons. Simpson and Rubin read "The Fall of the House of Usher" as a prophecy of the future downfall of the slave South (Rubin, *Edge* 158–60; Simpson, "Southern Recovery" 2–5). Taking a broader perspective, Toni Morrison finds something of the American soul in Poe in the form of an "Africanist presence" (*Playing* 47). William Carlos Williams sees him as "the astounding, inconceivable growth of his locality" (226), a writer who "conceived the possibility, the sullen, volcanic inevitability of the *place*"; "[h]e was willing," Williams writes, "to go down and wrestle with its conditions, using every tool France, England, Greece could give him,—but to use them to original purpose" (225). Of course, Williams may have had his own aesthetic commitments, not Poe's, uppermost in his mind.

However, for all these writers, "place" is chiefly a matter of mind, soul, society, and culture as determinants of a genius loci. If we take this perspective, I suppose we could point out (agreeing fundamentally with Williams) that Poe's work is less placeless than it is broadly placed in terms of both time and culture. In other words, much of his work invokes cultures of empire that are generally northern or western European, sometimes trans(North)-Atlantic, sometimes Mediterranean, sometimes South Seas/Dutch East Indies. This shouldn't be surprising, not just because Poe was raised in a port city, but because most of his later haunts were along the Atlantic Seaboard, from Boston down to Sullivan's Island—all places closely tied to ports that saw trade from England, northern and western Europe, the Mediterranean, Africa, and the South Seas, representing a good deal of the known world in that period. As for time, Poe's imagined temporalities range from the late Middle Ages to the early modern period and his own nineteenth century. Perhaps it is not so much that Poe is a writer outside of time and place but that his sense of time and place possesses a broadly Eurocentric and transatlantic historical depth and imperial geographical scope. In other words, the "locality" (to borrow again from Williams) of Poe's imagination is a geographical, temporal, and cultural crossroads, remarkable for its aggregations of tropes and allusions relevant to many times and places. The child of a city of merchants, Poe was himself a kind of merchant, if by that we mean an agent of exchange.

In fact, he has given us a good deal of work set clearly in specific places—"The Gold Bug" (Sullivan's Island), "A Tale of the Ragged Mountains" (a mountain outcropping not far from Charlottesville), "The Premature Burial" (Richmond and the James River area), "The Journal of Julius Rodman" (the American West). Other tales, such as "The Man That Was Used Up," seem to be set in places generally American. "The Man of the Crowd" is set in London, and the events of "The Murders in the Rue Morgue," of course, take place in Paris, while "The Cask of Amontillado" is set in Italy, "Ligeia" around the Mediterranean and the Rhine (before the story moves to England after Ligeia's death and the narrator's marriage to Rowena), and "A Descent into the Mael-ström" in Norway. *The Narrative of Arthur Gordon Pym* takes us from Nantucket to the Antarctic in company with an American crew, describing a project of exploration and terror.

Maybe we are, today, more like Poe (or he is more like us) than we have realized. First, most of us are aware that we do not live in a social world that is "organic" in the sense Charles Reagan Wilson means, and in that awareness we may well have something in common with Poe and others of his generation in the United States. Neither the society Poe inhabited nor the worlds he imagined were organic in the sense of social, economic, or cultural stability. Richmond and the entire Eastern Seaboard were a crossroads where people from many different places and traditions were circulating. Moreover, the era he lived in, as I have indicated, straddled the divide between early modern and nineteenth-century temporalities—the early modern era is said to end around 1815, although, as we know, endings, like beginnings, are often long and slow. Not only was the South (as we have understood it as a distinctive region) just coming into existence during Poe's lifetime, but the U.S. national identity was also under construction. One thing we can say for certain is that if Poe's narrators seem estranged from the world around them in one way or another—alien or isolate, sometimes the final or only or alienated descendant of an unnamed or unknown lineage—it is because they are more often poised at the end rather than at the beginning of a tradition or lineage, and this itself makes Poe somewhat unusual in an era of American literary nationalism.

Second, our rethinking of the concept of place in the spirit of our own more ecologically attuned age signals a new imperative. To know one's place deeply is not only to know its human history but also to know something of the natural world one inhabits and its history—to know oneself in terms of bioregion and the almost inconceivably interwoven realities of ecosystems. In the classic 1969 anthology *The Subversive Science*, Paul Shepard writes of the outer layer of skin as being "ecologically like a pond surface or a forest soil, not a shell so much as a delicate interpenetration" (2). And in his essay "Beyond Ecology," Neil Evernden asks, "Where do you draw the line between one creature and another? Where does one organism stop and another begin? Is there even a boundary between you and the non-living world, or will the atoms in this page be a part of your body tomorrow? How, in short, can you make any sense out of the concept of man as a discrete entity?" (17). Poe suggests something of this sort in "The Colloquy of Monos and Una." Monos—speaking after death—reminds his interlocutor, Una, that there are "principles which should have taught our race to submit to the guidance of the natural laws, rather than attempt their control" (609). But we would not listen, and intellect, system, abstraction reign. When Monos dies, though, a change occurs: "The consciousness of being had grown hourly more indistinct, and that of mere locality had, in great measure, usurped its position. The idea of entity was becoming merged in that of place. The narrow space immediately surrounding what had been the body"—the earth surrounding the coffin—"was now growing to be the body itself" (616).

I want to foreground this ecological sense of place in Poe's work. And although I focus mostly on Poe's Upper South world, I want to emphasize that I have defined "locality" in this Upper South in terms of the crossroads, and Poe himself as an agent of exchange among cultures and times, and to emphasize that his orientation is toward endings rather than beginnings. So, in the spirit of the "crossroads local," I'd like to call your attention to a major climate event in April 1815, only a few months before the young Poe traveled with the Allans to England in July 1815. This was the great eruption of Mount Tambora on the Indonesian island of Sumbawa— an eruption more violent and more devastating than that of Krakatoa in 1883, and, it has been said, the worst eruption in ten thousand years of earth's history, which makes it even more devastating than the eruption of Mount Vesuvius in AD 79. Although science was not sufficiently advanced in 1815 to recognize the global impact, we have since learned that the climate effects of the Tambora event were felt as far away as England and Virginia, as ash and gases circled the globe. Eighteen sixteen was known as "the year without a summer"—there was frost in Virginia in August. Thomas Jefferson worried not only about the impact of that unusual year on agriculture at Monticello but about the impact a potential cooling of the American climate might have on his agrarian ideal for the future United States itself (Wood 206). In fact, a worldwide disruption of the growing seasons resulted in widespread famine throughout Europe and America.

The aftereffects of the eruption have been examined by students of Romanticism in art and literature—an atmospheric darkening, red sunsets, and, oddest of all, a temporary melting of the Arctic ice caps that led some British scientists and explorers interested in a Northwest Passage to enthusiastically present the case for that passage having opened (Wood 123). These aftereffects have been established as an influence on the work of J. M. W. Turner (among other painters); on Lord Byron's poem "Darkness," with its failing fires, its war, its famine; on John Keats's ode "To Autumn," said to record the emotional (and aesthetic) release with which Keats witnessed the first year of good harvests in 1819 after the cold and dark of the previous three years; on Mary Shelley's *Frankenstein*, with its association between loneliness and the Arctic; and, importantly, on the trajectory of Romanticism itself (Campbell et al. 43).

It is possible that something of Poe's dark Romanticism (gloomy interiors, shadowy realms, melancholia) might be traceable to the three years of darkness that followed the eruption of Tambora, as is the case with the British Romantics. One thing we can say with some certainty is that Poe's aesthetics of the natural world gravitates toward darkness and is often associated with melancholy, with terror, and with death. He would not have had to look far beyond his own home landscape for sources.

For example, L. Moffitt Cecil finds similarities between Poe's description of the strange water on the island of Tsalal in *The Narrative of Arthur Gordon Pym* and the water in some of Virginia's mineral springs. Cecil argues that the strangeness itself (for example, that the water did not appear "limpid," although it was; that it was neither "colourless, nor was it of any one uniform colour," appearing in varied shades of purple; that it "was made up of a number of distinct veins, each of a distinct hue," which "did not commingle" but nevertheless cohered [Poe, *Pym* 155]) has a parallel in writings by naturalists on the subject of Virginia for the *Southern Literary Messenger* (Cecil 399). And he conjectures that the chasms Pym and Peters encounter on Tsalal, along with the blackness of its inhabitants (blackness extending even to their teeth), might have been inspired by the Heth coal mines only twelve miles from Richmond (402). In addition, given that, thanks to the cotton gin, the cotton industry was replacing tobacco as the South's primary cash crop during Poe's lifetime, the ashy "whiteness" that Pym and Peters see around them as they float southward away from Tsalal could easily have had its imaginative origin in Poe's experience of the natural world southward from Virginia.

Burton Pollin has looked at Poe's use of the Dismal Swamp in "Philosophy of Furniture," where Poe recommends that Americans decorate their walls with paintings that are similar to John G. Chapman's *The Lake of the Dismal Swamp* in their darkness. Joan Dayan finds evidence of the Great Dismal Swamp in Poe's "Silence—A Fable"; ostensibly Poe is writing of a "dreary region in Libya, by the borders of the river Zaire" (Poe 195), but the descriptions are more appropriate to the Great Dismal Swamp region, where "the tall primeval trees rock eternally hither and thither with a crashing and mighty sound," where "strange poisonous flowers lie writhing," and where "the gray clouds rush westwardly forever, until they roll, a cataract, over the fiery wall of the horizon" (Poe 195–196). Libya is, by the way, about 90 percent desert, and the "river Zaire" is actually in the Congo, well away from Libya, which borders the Mediterranean.

The association of the swamp with Africa was widespread, given its renown as a refuge for the self-emancipated from among the South's enslaved population. Dayan points out that Poe's "most unnatural fictions are bound to the works of natural history that are so much a part of their origination," which is true. Natural history was a subject that interested many educated people during Poe's era. But her goal is to explore the subject of slavery, "the entangled metaphysics of romance and servitude," and when she notes "the methodical transactions in which [Poe] revealed the threshold separating humanity from animality" (241), she narrows her focus to that end.

My project is different, and I look at Poe's references to the natural world somewhat more literally—in other words, I prefer not to leap so quickly to the figurative or allegorical dimensions of his allusions, although I do plan to leap.

Poe's threshold does not, as Dayan argues, merely draw the human and animal into relationship; it troubles the distinction between human and vegetable, between human and inorganic worlds. Poe had a particular interest in botany and first took up its study during his schooldays in England. His work is filled with both the flora and the fauna of his Upper South world.

In his early work we find the clearest evidence that he was drawing from the wetlands around him in Virginia and North Carolina. It is widely agreed that his 1827 poem "The Lake—To—" is set around Lake Drummond in the Dismal Swamp, a "wild" and "dim" lake surrounded by "black rock" and "tall pines," the site of "terror" and "tremulous delight" (85–86) in the face of its landscape of death. We see similar imagery in "Fairyland" from 1829, with its references to "dim vales," "shadowy floods," "cloudy-looking woods," and "tempests" (140–41). Even his reference to "a yellow Albatross" (141) in this poem is not entirely outside the realm of natural history. Perhaps he encountered the image in some reading, but it is not improbable that the Chesapeake Bay and Albemarle Sound regions would have hosted an occasional "yellow Albatross," that is, a yellow-nosed albatross blown northward in a storm. We know that albatrosses did inhabit the Mid-Atlantic and Upper South areas at one time, thanks to the discovery of their fossils.

In "Introduction" (1831), Poe refers to "a painted paroquet," a "familiar bird" with "a most knowing eye" that taught the poet to speak as he (a child) lay in the "wildwood" while years rolled by "like tropic storms" (156). It is entirely possible that Poe has the Carolina paroquet (or parakeet or parrot—the names seem to have been used interchangeably in Poe's day) in mind. He might have observed the bird in the wild, or perhaps he saw it in John James Audubon's *Birds of America*, which began publication in 1827. In the same poem, Poe references "Condor years" (157). Although the condor no longer inhabits the Upper South and Mid-Atlantic, the American condor could be found on the East Coast during Poe's lifetime. His reference to the "greybeard" (158) in this poem is not an allusion to an old man—it most likely denotes the Grancy Greybeard (or *Chionanthus virginicus*), a kind of fringetree native to the Southeast and Mid-Atlantic.

Note, too, his poems' many allusions to the unusual climate: in "Fairyland," "Alone," "Dream-Land," and "Introduction," he references lightning, thunder, storms, clouds, and torrents. For all the transfigurations of Poe's imagination at work on the natural world—and I do not want to discount his powerful transfigurative imagination—the natural world of his Upper South home in its most literal dimensions is also present, and meaningful, in his work.

As to the sentience of the vegetable world, in "The Fall of the House of Usher" Poe references Dr. Thomas Percival, who was most famous for his work on medical ethics and who put forward the idea of vegetable sentience in *Speculations on the Perceptive Power of Vegetables: Addressed to the Literary and Philosophical Society of Manchester*. In this 1785 pamphlet, Percival spends some time discussing a certain "native of North Carolina": "The upper joint consists of two lobes, each of which is semi-oval in its form, with a margin furnished with stiff hairs; which embrace each other, when they close from any irritation. The surfaces of these lobes are covered with small red glands, which probably secrete some sweet liquor, tempting to the taste, but fatal to the lives of insects: For, the moment the poor animal alights upon these parts, the two lobes rise up, grasp it forcibly, lock the rows of spines together, and squeeze it to death" (8–9). Today we call this North Carolina native the Venus flytrap. Percival proposes that its movement, spontaneous and based on instinct, proves his point, which is that the movement of plants in response to external stimulation makes them more like animals than we have recognized. Don't those drops of "sweet liquor" from the "small red glands" put one in mind of that moment in "Ligeia" when "ruby colored" drops fall from nowhere into the cup from which Lady Rowena is drinking (325), precipitating Rowena's death and the resurrection of Ligeia herself, the narrator's first wife?

In all these examples, we see evidence of Poe's continuing interest in that "threshold," as Dayan puts it, that not only divides "humanity from animality" but also links us to the world of plants through vegetable sentience. There is evidence of these entanglements in Poe's signature aesthetic tropes, the arabesque and the grotesque. The arabesque, after all, is a decorative art form that interlocks figures of flora and fauna in leaf, tendril, wing, and bird; the grotesque is an art of the hybrid—human, animal, plant, the organic and the inorganic united in a monstrous (or monstrously beautiful) body.

Ultimately Poe's aesthetic positions the human subject, and human subjectivity itself, as part of a universal order in which even the soul is matter—matter refined, but matter nonetheless. In one of Poe's stories, "Mesmeric Revelation," a Mr. Vankirk, close to death, is "mesmerized" and then questioned, in his liminal state, about the afterlife. When asked whether God is immaterial, Mr. Vankirk replies that "There is no immateriality. [. . .] That which is not matter, is not at all—unless qualities are things" (1033). He goes on to explain that there are "*gradations* of matter of which man knows nothing; the grosser impelling the finer, the finer pervading the grosser"; he continues, "These gradations of matter increase in rarity or fineness, until we arrive at a matter *unparticled*—without particles—indivisible—*one*. [. . .] The ultimate, or unparticled matter, not only permeates all things, but impels all things—and thus *is* all things within itself. This matter is God. What men attempt to embody in the word 'thought,' is this matter in motion" (1033). He then ranks matter as follows, from coarse to fine: "a metal, a piece of wood, a drop of water, the atmosphere, a gas, caloric, electricity, the luminiferous ether" (1034). He asks us to think of a matter even more refined than "the luminiferous ether," which we might call spirit but is nevertheless material. In short, spirit is matter.

We can best understand Poe's great subject, terror, through the lens of this understanding of the natural world, of place and matter, and argue that, in Poe, terror *is* the materiality of the soul and the sentience of the natural world, a sentience he seems to have felt intensely. It reflects, I argue, that "interpenetration," as Paul Shepard terms it, between "epidermis" and "forest soil" (2), and the question Neil Evernden asks: "Is there [. . .] a boundary between you and the non-living world, or will the atoms in this page be a part of your body tomorrow? How, in short, can you make any sense out of the concept of man as a discrete entity?" (17).

Poe entered "Mr. Jefferson's University" in 1826, a few months before Thomas Jefferson's death on July 4 of that year. He joined the Jefferson Literary and Debating Society not long after his matriculation, and it is likely that he knew Jefferson's *Notes on the State of Virginia*.

In Query VII of that book, Jefferson observes that the elevation of Monticello "affords an opportunity of seeing a phaenomenon which is rare at land, though frequent at sea. The seamen call it *looming*. [. . .] Its principal effect is to make distant objects appear larger, in opposition to the general law of vision, by which they are diminished." He continues: "I knew an instance, at York town, from whence the water prospect eastwardly is without termination, wherein a canoe with three men, at a great distance, was taken for a ship with its three masts." He then goes on to recount the story of the phenomenon as it affects Willis Mountain, viewed from Monticello: "There is a solitary mountain about 40 miles off, in the South, whose natural shape, as presented to view there, is a regular cone; but, by the effect of looming, it sometimes subsides almost totally into the horizon; sometimes it rises more acute and more elevated; sometimes it is hemispherical; and sometimes its sides are perpendicular, its top flat, and as broad as its base. In short it assumes at times the most whimsical shapes, and all these perhaps successively in the same morning" (87–88).

Jefferson does not know the cause of this land-based form of "looming" but observes that it happens only in the mornings and that the objects affected are "at least 40 or 50 miles distant." He emphasizes that it is different from the kind of "looming" that we see "on the water," and he discounts "refraction" as its cause: "Refraction will not account for this metamorphosis," he writes; "[t]hat only changes the proportions of length and breadth, base and altitude, preserving the general outlines. Thus it may make a circle appear elliptical, raise or depress a cone, but by none of its laws, as yet developed, will it make a circle appear a square, or a cone a sphere" (88).

I cannot read the preceding passage without thinking of Edgar Allan Poe. Aside from the issues of "refraction" and "metamorphosis" in general, which are so central to Poe's work, I am reminded of the last pages of *The Narrative of Arthur Gordon Pym*, in which Pym, his half–Native American/half-white friend Dirk Peters, and Nu-Nu, their captive and a native of the Antarctic island of Tsalal, are floating southward after having escaped death at the hands of Nu-Nu's compatriots on Tsalal. They make their escape in a canoe, and as they travel farther southward, the water becomes warmer and milky, there is an odd ashy material in the air, and ahead they discern vapor that Pym likens to "a limitless cataract, rolling silently into the sea from some immense and far distant rampart in the heaven" (197). As they float closer, "there came rushing and mighty, but soundless winds," until finally, the last entry in Pym's journal reads:

> The darkness had materially increased, relieved only by the glare of the water thrown back from the white curtain before us. Many gigantic and pallidly white birds flew continuously now from beyond the veil. [. . .] And now we rushed into the embraces of the cataract, where a chasm threw itself open to receive us. But there arose in our pathway a shrouded human figure, very far larger in its proportions than any dweller among men. And the hue of the skin of the figure was of the perfect whiteness of the snow. (198)

With this passage, the account ends. The figure looming in the men's path has been read in any number of ways. It might have been an actual human (perhaps a giant from the Hollow Earth, Hollow Earth theory being popular at the time); a carving of a human figure or something else; the figurehead of a ship; or, given Jefferson's passage quoted above, a person or object that is actually much smaller, such as someone standing in a canoe or something of that sort.

I am most persuaded by these last two suggestions. There have been two relevant patterns in the novel—a pattern of deceptive appearances, and a pattern of extreme desperation followed by rescue; and Pym and Peters, we know from the retrospective structure of the novel, do survive the experience. Pym returns to begin an account of events but dies before it is completed, leaving his journal and responsibility for completing the narrative in the hands of a gentleman from Richmond, a certain Mr. Poe. Unfortunately, Mr. Poe's efforts to reach Dirk Peters for information about how he and Pym survived fail, so readers are left to conjecture about the nature of the "shrouded human figure."[1]

Of course, "looming" has another, more metaphorical meaning. When something "looms" before you, it not only manifests in a larger form than expected but also has a prophetic dimension. In other words, it can signify something arriving in time: "the deadline for a decision loomed"—that kind of thing. Both meanings signify in *Pym*.

If we pursue this last suggestion, we might conjecture that at the end of *Pym*, Poe is alluding, in 1838, to the development of an American future very different from the one Jefferson envisioned in the 1780s when he undertook to write *Notes on the State of Virginia*.

How might Jefferson's *Notes* have been read by Edgar Allan Poe? In 1780, François Barbé-Marbois, the secretary to the French legation in Philadelphia, posed to members of the Continental Congress the series of questions that led to the *Notes*. These questions had to do with the prospects of the new nation and were designed to elicit information for a European audience with some reservations about those prospects. Jefferson received the queries, and *Notes on the State of Virginia* appeared in 1785. *Notes* took up subjects ranging from the boundaries of Virginia to the state's "Histories, memorials, and state-papers," but I want to focus on Jefferson's comments on the mountains in Query IV.

Here Jefferson situates his reader "on a very high point of land," with the Shenandoah on the right and the Potomac on the left, both rivers "in quest of a passage" and violently meeting to "rush together against the mountain, rend it asunder, and pass off to the sea." He goes on:

> But the distant finishing which nature has given to the picture is of a very different character. It is a true contrast to the foreground. It is as placid and delightful, as that is wild and tremendous. For the mountain being cloven asunder, she presents to your eye, through the cleft, a small catch of smooth blue horizon, at an infinite distance in the plain country, inviting you, as it were, from the riot and tumult roaring around, to pass through the breach and participate of the calm below. Here the eye ultimately composes itself; and that way too the road happens actually to lead. (21)

Jefferson describes a natural world within which the prospects of the New World nation will be like that "small catch of smooth blue horizon" to the West, however "infinite" in distance from the present moment.

Robert Lawson-Peebles points out that Jefferson "wished to understand and control" the natural world and that he was especially inclined toward an "aerial view," the view of a remote observer, "looking down on America, as if from a great height, and imposing order upon it" (167). The natural world of Poe's imagination could not be more different. We have only to consider some of his titles to discern what Poe's world looks like: "A Descent into the Maelström," "MS. Found in a Bottle," "The Fall of the House of Usher." Poe's natural world is a world of descents and falls, in which one can be cast adrift, or lost.

I stated earlier that I did not want to move too quickly to a figurative or metaphorical reading, but clearly at this point I'm doing just that. And I'd like to continue in this vein with "A Tale of the Ragged Mountains." In this story an un-named narrator tells of Augustus Bedloe, who is under the care of a physician and mesmerist, Dr. Templeton, whom Bedloe met years before at Saratoga. At the time of the events of the story, in the fall of 1827, Bedloe is "singularly tall and thin," his arms and legs "exceedingly long and emaciated," his forehead "broad and low," his mouth "large and flex-ible," and his teeth "more wildly uneven [. . .] than I [the narrator] had ever before seen teeth in a human head." Bed-loe has a "bloodless" complexion and a pronounced stoop. His smile is "one of profound melancholy—of a phaseless and unceasing gloom." And his eyes are "abnormally large, and round like those of a cat." They even behave like a cat's eyes—expanding and dilating with the light as in "the feline tribe." But "[i]n moments of excitement the orbs grew bright to a degree almost inconceivable; seeming to emit luminous rays, not of a reflected but of an intrinsic lustre, as does a candle or the sun; yet their ordinary condition was so totally vapid, filmy, and dull, as to convey the idea of the eyes of a long-interred corpse" (940). Augustus implies that he was not always so unattractive—that he used to possess consider-able beauty but has been transformed by neuralgia into the ugly creature he now is (940–41).

One morning in November, in the period Americans term "Indian Summer"—an important detail—the "young gentle-man" (at least at times he seems young, while at other times the narrator tells us he could imagine Bedloe being a hundred years old) sets off on a morning ramble to the Ragged Moun-tains, not far from Charlottesville. Note that this excursion is set only a year after the death of Jefferson and not long after Poe himself had left "Mr. Jefferson's University." Poe himself is said to have walked in the Ragged Mountains when he was in residence in Charlottesville.

Bedloe is walking along when he spies a gorge he has never seen before. He enters the gorge and is immediately taken with the "absolutely virgin" solitude and "dreary des-

olation" (942) of the place, which is filled with the charac-
teristic smoke of the mountains in that season. He cannot
see very far ahead—one might suggest that his strange feline
eyes do not "compose themselves" as Jefferson imagines they
would in looking westward. He perceives a bright and animated natural world around him, however: "In the quivering
of a leaf—in the hue of a blade of grass—in the shape of a
trefoil—in the humming of a bee—in the gleaming of a dew-
drop," and so on, "there came a whole universe of suggestion—a gay and motley train of rhapsodical and immethodi-
cal thought" (943).

After walking for several hours, he finds himself increasingly unable to see ahead. Afraid of plunging into "some
abyss" or of encountering the "uncouth and fierce races of
men who tenanted their groves and caverns" (943)—a detail that might suggest either the Native Americans (who had
been forced out by that point) or the "uncouth and fierce"
poor whites who lived in that area at the time—Bedloe suddenly hears "the loud beating of a drum," which is surprising enough (since, he tells us, no drum had ever been heard
in these hills). It is followed by "a wild rattling or jingling
sound, as if of a bunch of large keys—and upon the instant,"
Bedloe recounts, "a dusky-visaged and half-naked man" appears, running past Bedloe "with a shriek" and carrying "an
assemblage of steel rings" that he shakes as he runs. And as
if that isn't enough, Bedloe discerns a hyena in pursuit of the
man (943–44).

Bedloe thinks he must be dreaming. After dashing cold
spring water onto his face, he continues on his way, "a new
man" (944). Surely Poe's satirical intent vis-à-vis Jefferson's
nationalistic rhetoric of optimism is clear at this point—there
is nothing whatsoever that is "new" about Bedloe. When he
sits down beneath a tree and discovers it to be a palm tree (in
the Virginia mountains!), he is understandably startled.

This is apparently where the interest of the story, for most
readers, begins. Bedloe is transported to an "Eastern-looking

city" full of minarets, shrines, silks, muslins, closely veiled women, rich marketplaces—a scene out of the Arabian tales. There are elephants, "holy filleted bulls," and "vast legions of the filthy but sacred ape [. . .] chattering and shrieking" and climbing all over the minarets and oriels (945).

Templeton and the narrator have been listening as Bedloe tells the story of his "singular" expedition earlier that day, and Templeton, impatient after Bedloe has digressed into some philosophical musings about the nature of the experience, interjects, "[P]roceed. You arose and descended into the city" (946).

Bedloe continues according to Templeton's directive. Remember that Templeton is a mesmerist, and Bedloe his patient—a remarkably susceptible one who can be put into a trance very easily, even when he is not in the presence of Dr. Templeton. Bedloe goes on to describe a fierce battle, the escape of "an effeminate-looking person" from a palace by means of a rope constructed of the turbans of his entourage, and then his own death by poisoned arrow to the temple (947).

Bedloe continues:

> For many minutes [. . .] my sole sentiment—my sole feeling— was that of darkness and nonentity, with the consciousness of death. At length there seemed to pass a violent and sudden shock through my soul, as if of electricity. With it came the sense of elasticity and of light. This latter I felt—not saw. In an instant I seemed to rise from the ground. But I had no bodily, no visible, audible, or palpable presence. [. . .] The city was in comparative repose. Beneath me lay my corpse, with the arrow in my temple, the whole head greatly swollen and disfigured. (947–48)

He is then transported back to the Ragged Mountains: "When I had attained that point of the ravine in the mountains, at which I had encountered the hyena, I again experienced a shock as of a galvanic battery; the sense of weight, of volition, of substance, returned. I became my original self, and bent my steps eagerly homewards" (948).

The mesmerist is oddly affected by the tale, and we soon learn why. He shows Bedloe a portrait, apparently of Bedloe himself, but drawn in 1780, almost fifty years earlier! Templeton explains that it is the portrait of a friend, Mr. Oldeb, whom he had known in Calcutta, "during the administration of Warren Hastings" (949), the first British governor-general of India. Templeton goes on to reveal that the events Bedloe described took place in Benares, India, under the administration of Hastings, and that the "effeminate person" escaping via the ladder made of turbans was Cheyte Sing, a local ruler from whom Hastings had exacted funds. The battle in which Bedloe participated was the battle of the British (led by Hastings) against the Indians, a battle in which Templeton's friend of the portrait, the one with the remarkable resemblance to Bedloe, died of an arrow to the temple.

Not long after recounting his story to Templeton and the narrator, Bedloe dies in a similar way. It seems he had contracted a head cold during his visit to the Ragged Mountains, and in treating him with medicinal leeches, Dr. Templeton inadvertently attaches a poisonous leech to Bedloe's right temple, causing his death. The writer of the death notice in a Charlottesville newspaper informs the reader that one can always recognize the "poisonous sangsue of Charlottesville" (in actuality, there is no such thing) "by its blackness, and especially by its writhing or vermicular motions, which very nearly resemble those of a snake" (950). Recall that Bedloe describes the arrow coming toward him in the Benares scene as black and writhing.

There are simply too many counterpoints to Jefferson's optimistic nationalism in Poe's tale to be accidental. Jefferson looks into a landscape of regular ridges leading west toward space and serenity, the end of chaos; Poe sends Bedloe into the "Ragged Mountains" and directs Bedloe's attention to an "Eastern-looking city" that "swarmed with inhabitants" and was clearly in the midst of an uprising (945).[2] Jefferson's imagined eye "composes itself" (21); what Bedloe sees with his odd, catlike eyes discomposes him. Jefferson's vision of pastoral innocence is countered by Poe's allusions to the corruptions of British colonialism and the prescient suggestion, hard to ignore, that the American project also lends itself to such violence.

The local details are themselves suggestive: Bedloe tells us first that no drum had ever been heard in the Ragged Mountains. How could that possibly be? The area of the Ragged Mountains was inhabited for years by the Monacan tribes of Native Americans. Today the headquarters of the Monacan Nation is about fifty miles from Charlottesville. Surely the running man who first appears in "A Tale of the Ragged Mountains" must have struck the readers of Poe's day as Native American; how apposite it is that he signals the interpolation of a story of Great Britain's colonialism on the Indian subcontinent into what is so erroneously presumed to be the most "virgin" (942) of American places, as if to announce an American future quite different from the one Jefferson imagines in *Notes on the State of Virginia*.

Could there be in Poe's "Tale of the Ragged Mountains" an engagement—however metamorphosed—with the subject of U.S. history in relation to the Native American? J. Gerald Kennedy, Michael J. S. Williams, and Maria Karafilis all think so (Kennedy 19–20; Williams 57–58; Karafilis 18). In 1830 Congress passed the Indian Removal Act, and the subsequent Treaty of New Echota established May 1838 as the deadline for removal. That is only six years before the initial publication of Poe's story. Surely it is significant that Poe sets a story dealing with the violence of British colonial power in India within an American world, a place where "dusky-visaged" is more likely to reference American Indians than inhabitants of the Indian subcontinent, and where "Indian Summer" (which is when Bedloe sets out on his ramble through the Ragged Mountains) would certainly have been familiar to his nineteenth-century readers as a way to reference that moment in November when, so it is said, Native

Americans took one final opportunity to attack the colonists before the snows set in.

We find traces of Native American culture in *The Narrative of Arthur Gordon Pym* as well. Quite apart from the fact that Pym's friend Dirk Peters is biracial, the events of the last pages of *Pym* take place on the island of Tsalal. Although Poe's imaginary island is usually understood as Black territory, its name is similar to the Cherokee word *tsalaki*, which means "Cherokee," and there was a Cherokee chief named Tsali who, in the 1830s during Indian removal, killed American soldiers. Poe's novel was published in 1838, and it is quite likely that indigeneity is more at issue in that text than slavery and the prospect of rebellion by enslaved people. The natives of Tsalal are not, in fact, enslaved. In "The Name of the Nation," a short essay published in *Graham's* in 1846, Poe suggests that our country be renamed "The United States of Appalachia" because it is "distinctive" (unlike "America," which applies to Central and South America too) and because the name "Appalachia" is "indigenous, springing from one of the most magnificent and distinctive features of the country itself." He adds that "in employing this word we do honor to the Aborigines, whom, hitherto, we have at all points unmercifully despoiled, assassinated and dishonored" (600), which is comparable to what is happening to the Indians in Bedloe's vision.[3]

CHAPTER THREE

Backwater

Westering

> I used to think backwater meant
> Remote or backward, out of date,
> a place of stagnant poverty.
> But found the term in history meant
> across the mountain watershed
> where rivers run the other way
> to west to wilderness, to where
> the future waits to open out
> its shining promise, destiny.
> Backwater meant new water then,
> where greatness waited tilted toward
> the sunset rivers of hope where
> the worst of us, the very worst
> of all, might find a seventh chance.
>
> —ROBERT MORGAN, "BACKWATER"

This powerful poem by the North Carolina poet Robert Morgan embeds hope in melancholy. Contrary to nationalist mythmaking, narratives of westering are as likely to record melancholy stories of loss and failure—suggested here in the imagery of "sunset rivers," "might," and "seventh chance"— as they are to record the "shining promise" of hope.

In the previous chapter I explored the Virginia origins of Poe's melancholy natural world of swamps, storms, mountains, cliffs, forests, waterfalls, and gorges—the dizzying height and deep abyss of his mindscape as a conversation with, and troubling of, the New World optimism of the Revolutionary era, represented by Thomas Jefferson.

In this chapter I'd like to pick up on the troubling of New World optimism and look a little more closely at westering in the work of Elizabeth Madox Roberts, Cormac McCarthy (briefly), and Toni Morrison. All are writers of "the North of the South," if in different ways. Roberts is from a Kentucky family, while McCarthy comes from Rhode Islanders who moved to Tennessee to work with the Tennessee Valley Authority. Morrison was born in Ohio, but her parents were from the Deep South (her mother was from Alabama and her father was from Georgia). Her imagined world, wherever it is geographically, is always "South," if by that we can mean that it is shaped by, colored by, and fundamentally inseparable from the region we know as the U.S. South. The natural world is central in the work of all three writers, and all engage with "westering" in the predominant mode of melancholy.

In the 1820s, Captain Basil Hall toured the United States. While in South Carolina, he visited an orphan asylum:

> While looking at this Orphan Asylum, my attention was called to some curious features of American society, which contra-distinguish it from that of old countries. All the world in that busy land is more or less on the move, and as the whole community is made up of units, amongst which there is little of the principle of cohesion, they are perpetually dropping out of one another's sight, in the wide field over which they are scattered. Even the connexions of the same family are soon lost sight of — the children glide away from their parents, long before their manhood ripens; — brothers and sisters stream off to the right and left, mutually forgetting one another, and being forgotten by their families. (165–66)

So much for the famous southern sense of place, sense of family, depth of memory. If we believe him, the national reality, even in South Carolina, where Hall made these observations in the early years of the Republic, seems to have been forgetfulness, loss of place, loss of memory.

In the preceding passage, Hall draws on a familiar representation of the "field of memory," taken from Augustine's *Confessions*, in which Augustine describes memory as being

> like a great field or a spacious palace, a storehouse for countless images of all kinds which are conveyed to it by the senses. In it are stored away all the thoughts by which we enlarge upon or diminish or modify in any way the perceptions at which we arrive through the senses, and it also contains anything else that has been entrusted to it for safe keeping, until such time as these things are swallowed up and buried in forgetfulness. (6)

One of the most conventional strategies for remembering comes from this passage from Book X of the *Confessions*. As an aid to remembering, the would-be rememberer imaginatively places specific images around an imagined location, such as a palace, a city, or some other well-known site. Remembering then becomes a process of "collecting," that is, "recollecting" these images or words as one moves through the familiar rooms, streets, or pathways. Orators used to memorize long speeches using this technique. Apart from the fact that this mnemonic strategy underscores connections among places, memory, and identity that are as old as ancient Greece, suggesting that to lose the places of one's life is a challenge to the memories of one's life, it also makes clear that memory is active, embodied, and essentially a relationship with both the internal and external worlds.

For anyone living in the twenty-first century, the most striking feature of Augustine's description of memory may be the apparent stability of the "great field," "spacious palace," and "storehouse" to which we can "entrust" our memories because we can trust them to remain "until such time as these things are swallowed up and buried in forgetfulness." Augustine's passage has a luminosity associated with a world in which time moves slowly. It evokes a world in which fields stood a good chance of remaining untrampled and palaces could be left standing for generations, but maybe this aura of slow time is simply a product of the canonization of Augustine—not to sainthood, but into the canon of "the best of Western thought," with all its associations of permanence.

Surely it is relevant that Augustine, African and born in what is now Algeria, died at the hands of the Vandals in the siege of the place where he wrote these words. Vandals no doubt overrode the fields, emptied the storehouses, and raided the palace—displacing the images, relics, and icons that constituted memories and leaving them scattered all over these and other unfamiliar places.

What followed must have been the fragmentation of cultural memory, a form of forgetting. Augustine feels so relevant today (and has, in fact, been the foundation for a tradition of modern autobiographical writing) because of this. In some ways his story is very modern.

Deleuze and Guattari write that modernity leaves nothing whole:

> We live today in the age of partial objects, bricks that have been shattered to bits, and leftovers. We no longer believe in the myth of the existence of fragments that, like pieces of an antique statue, are merely waiting for the last one to be turned up, so that they may all be glued back together to create a unity that is precisely the same as the original unity. We no longer believe in a primordial totality that once existed, or in a final totality that awaits us at some future date. We no longer believe in the dull gray outlines of a dreary, colorless dialectic of evolution, aimed at forming a harmonious whole out of heterogeneous bits by rounding off their rough edges. We believe only in totalities that are peripheral. And if we discover such a totality alongside various separate parts, it is a whole *of* these particular parts but does not totalize them; it is a unity *of* all of these particular parts but does not unify them; rather it is added to them as a new part fabricated separately. (42)

Within this world of "partial objects," of "heterogeneous bits," modern writers are engaged in memory work in its broadest sense, and southern writers are no exception.

Elizabeth Madox Roberts is not well known today. Following the publication of her groundbreaking modernist novel *The Time of Man* in 1926, she was hailed as one of the major voices of American modernism. By the time of her death in 1941, she had published twelve books, among them novels, collections of short stories, and poetry collections.

The Time of Man is the story of Ellen Chesser, a Kentucky tenant farmer's wife and mother of several children who is never able to settle in one place for long. "It was," Roberts wrote, "[. . .] in the summer of 1919 that I began to think of the wandering tenant farmer of our region as offering a symbol for an Odyssey of Man as wanderer buffeted about by the fates and the weathers" (qtd. in Campbell and Foster 124). To my mind, *The Time of Man* doesn't so much tell the story of a man "buffeted about by the fates and the weathers" as it tells that of a woman buffeted about by a sorry excuse for a husband, who may be a barn burner, and the dreary reality of tenant farming. Nevertheless, Roberts evokes Ellen's consciousness, the natural world, and her circumstances in a lyrical style that gives her protagonist a mythic stature, and it is this feature of the novel that has received the most commentary.

At the end of the novel, Ellen and her children are following Jasper yet again, after he has suffered a humiliating beating at the hands of the Klan. He explains to Ellen that "I'll go somewheres far out of hearen of this place. I've done little that's amiss here, but still I'd have to go. I couldn't see my way to stay here and that's what I studied out all day. I aim to go far, so far that word from this place can't come there or is not likely" (378). Later, Ellen tells her children that they are off to "[s]ome better country. Our own place maybe. Our trees in the orchard. Our own land sometime. Our place to keep. . . ."—although this, the reader knows, is unlikely. It is a journey without destination on which they are bound: "They went a long way while the moon was still high above the trees, stopping only at some creek to water the beasts. They asked no question of the way but took their own turnings" (382). One can almost see them, like the dead, vanishing into the remote time and space of memory.

There is in these passages something of the kind of world Robert Morgan describes in "Backwater," a world of hope mixed with resignation, and something of the world that Cormac McCarthy conjures four decades later for another age. Surely Roberts is one of Cormac McCarthy's influences. In McCarthy's *Child of God*, Lester Ballard has watched his family farm sold off and proceeds to accumulate "property" in the form of the dead bodies of the women he has killed, which he houses deep in the caves around Knoxville. He too dreams of another world:

> He dreamt that night that he rode through woods on a low ridge. Below him he could see deer in a meadow where the sun fell on the grass. The grass was still wet and the deer stood in it to their elbows. He could feel the spine of the mule rolling under him and he gripped the mule's barrel with his legs. Each leaf that brushed his face deepened his sadness and dread. Each leaf he passed he'd never pass again. They rode over his face like veils, already some yellow, their veins like slender bones where the sun shone through them. He had resolved himself to ride on for he could not turn back and the world that day was as lovely as any day that ever was and he was riding to his death. (170–71)

The reception of Cormac McCarthy emphasizes the violence, the grotesque, but a glance at the criticism on Roberts's work reveals that, in spite of any number of different approaches, there is one apparent consensus: Elizabeth Madox Roberts is a writer who celebrates agrarian tradition and the pioneering resilience of her female protagonists. Of Ellen Chesser, one critic writes that "[i]t is only by consciously accepting the connection between history and the land to which she has intimately connected herself that Ellen begins to be able to embrace history as an expansive force of which she can make her own uses. This is a mastery that she increasingly develops as the novel moves toward its end" (LeRoy-Frazier 69). To me, though, such readings—which may inscribe familiar expectations (or desires) in connection with female subjectivities—appear somewhat desperate in their desire to minimize the violence and the melancholy of westering in the representation of women's experience.

In the face of this consensus, I want to go somewhat against the grain of criticism and focus not on the comforts of place and tradition, the resilience of Roberts's female protagonists, or the dream of national promise, but on violence and loss, melancholy, and forgetting in Roberts's work. *The Time of Man*, *My Heart and My Flesh*, and *The Great Meadow* constitute a series, tracing a line of women from Diony Hall Jarvis, the pioneer ancestor of *The Great Meadow* who embarks from Virginia before the American Revolution, to Jarvis's twentieth-century descendants in *The Time of Man* and *My Heart and My Flesh*. I'll begin with the last novel in the series, published in 1930, because it is set at the earliest historical moment (and was actually begun in 1913, well before Roberts began writing *The Time of Man*).

The Great Meadow opens in 1774, on the eve of the American Revolution, in Albemarle, Virginia—we are back in the world of Thomas Jefferson. In the early twentieth century, historical novels dealing with the American Revolutionary period (like those set during the Civil War) were extremely popular, and many of them predictably attempted to hang a spread-eagle story of triumphant American nationalism on the common plot device of a romance and happy marriage between two worthy young people of British descent. Roberts plays variations on the theme. Diony Hall is a young woman from a prosperous family. She is strong, easily doing the work of the farm. She is literate and knows classical mythology. Her father reads Bishop Berkeley by the fireside, and she has absorbed the idealism of Berkeley's philosophy. She herself has a gift for words and a powerful imagination. She can imagine cities in the words she hears her father read, even though she has never seen a city (26). "Oh," she thinks, "to create rivers by knowing rivers. [. . .] Oh, to make a world out of chaos" (24). This is her dream—and I cannot help being reminded of McCarthy's Lester Ballard, who "[g]iven charge [. . .] would have made things more orderly in the woods and in men's souls" (*Child of God* 136), although Ballard's sense of "order" is that of a sociopath.

Diony is surprised and angered to learn that no part of Five Oaks, her family property in Albemarle, will come to her—that she must, her brother tells her, marry to "get a place" (18). So Diony does marry and is soon on the move with her new husband, Berk Jarvis, headed for Kentucky on that road from Richmond and Charlottesville running westward across the mountains toward what Jefferson saw as a "smooth blue horizon." Berk dreams of a "fine high house" (183).

At various stopping places the migrants meet up with others, and Diony, who is used to her father reading to her, listens instead to "ill-connected stories that finally fitted together into a merry, lewd recitative" (144). There are ballads sung, about the legendary Hannibal who would kill you as soon as look at you. When they arrive in Kentucky, they occupy a crude cabin in a clearing, with few others of their traditions around. They discover that the British Americans already there include a woman named Mistress Sovereigns—a significant name in a book that identifies the mind at one point as the "sovereign part of any man" (225)—but Mistress Sovereigns has had her tongue cut out by the Shawnees. Another woman's words are whipped from her in the November wind, "severed from her breath and flung outward without meaning" (195). Later she is killed and scalped.

Violence and forgetting are facts of life on the frontier. Soon Berk leaves on a mission of revenge against the Native Americans who have attacked their stockade, and Diony reminds him not to "forget what [he goes] for" (247). She knows that she is "a beginning before the beginning" (213), an interesting phrase to conjure with. Three years pass, and

Berk does not return. He is presumed dead. After the first year Diony gets married again, to another good man, Evan Muir, because survival demands it.

There is clearly something other than acceptance here. There is loss, terror, a deep melancholy associated most clearly in the choice she is compelled to make toward the end of the novel between her first husband, Berk, unexpectedly now returned, and her new husband. According to frontier practice, Roberts writes, a woman placed in such a situation has the right to choose, and the two men must accept, without objection, her decision (316–17).

They vie for her. Berk, sitting in the new house that Evan has built for Diony, tells the story of his captivity and his efforts to escape; Evan talks of the changes that "can come over a country in three years' time. [. . .] And over a man and a woman" (311). Evan has a farm, and Diony has had a child with him. Berk, only three years gone, seems already to belong to a vanished age associated with the movement of the first pioneers out of Virginia and into the west, but he continues to tell his story as if Evan has not spoken.

Diony chooses Berk. In him she remembers; she sees embodied the world she left behind. In choosing him, she lays claim to an earlier stage of history, the journey from Albemarle into the frontier. Somewhat like the characters in Poe's stories, Roberts's characters seem poised more at the end of things than at the beginning. Freud describes melancholy as a refusal or inability to give up the dead. There is something very Freudian in the way the dead man walks into Diony's house and takes up residence there, in the power of the stories he tells, in the way she welcomes him. He is a walking anachronism (his world being the world of Indian wars), and Diony's choice is a melancholic one.

It's a difficult decision she makes. In Tom, her child with Berk, she sees Albemarle and her people:

The child's hair was more yellow than Berk's and it curled lightly above the temples in the way of her own hair, but his skull was from Elvira. When he laughed, Betty came into the cabin; but when he sat puzzling over some bit of thread, studying closely some mystery of bent or knotted leather strand lost from her needle, his mouth slipped in pretty curves and angles and was the gift of Polly Brook. When she sang to him in the quiet of the winter dusk, finding song after song in her memory and making songs out of the matters in her father's books, then sometimes the child lifted his head suddenly and looked upward into her face, and it was Thomas Hall who looked there, as if his hand had been lifted to say "harken." (269)

Berk Jarvis, in his stories, and the child, in his body, carry memory, and in them she can reconstruct something of the past from the "partial objects" that remain. One critic writes that Diony "endeavors to discover herself by evaluating [her experiences] according to the 'Great Design of an Eternal Spirit,' which is detected in manifestations of Nature and events in the history of man" (Murphy 110). Again, it is not surprising that the violence, the suffering, and the melancholy should be so easily translated into a triumphalist narrative of the "history of man" culminating in a tale of American westering. This is the practice of our nationalist mythmaking. I do not believe it is Elizabeth Madox Roberts's practice.

The characters of the other two novels of the series (*The Time of Man* and *My Heart and My Flesh*) are Diony's descendants. At the beginning of *My Heart and My Flesh*, there appears, just briefly, a Luce Jarvis, a little girl who has somehow in mind a fine city named "Mome" that is oddly associated with mothers (who are themselves melancholy presences around her and who die with the end of their daughters' childhoods). In Roberts's papers there are notes referencing a projected "Book of Luce" dealing with this character who, in the twentieth century, has inherited or acquired in some way scattered relics from the past: pages from Diony's journal, now brown and dry as a "chip"; a pewter spoon with Diony's name on it, "shaped to fit into a mouth." She has plans that remind us of Diony's youthful desires and also Ellen Chesser's: "I will be something of my own right, of myself, I Luce Jarvis" (qtd. in Simpson, *Fable* 68).

Then Luce vanishes from the story, and another little girl, Theodosia Bell, takes center stage. *My Heart and My Flesh* is about Theodosia. Her life is a gothic terror. Theodosia's mother dies, and Theodosia's sister dies in childhood. We learn that her father has probably killed his wife by cheating on her and has fathered two biracial daughters—heavily named Lethe (forgetfulness, oblivion) and Americy—and a son, Stiggins (a "semi-idiot" stable boy [111]), all of whom live in abject poverty and degradation, unacknowledged. Theodosia's father threatens to rape Theodosia, forcing her to flee to the home of an old aunt, where she just barely survives by eating the cornbread cooked for the dogs, until she summons the will to hail a passing wagon and finds herself teaching school in the closest town and betrothed to a good farmer. Theodosia discovers her own resilience and enters into the life of an agrarian community, but ignoring the trauma that led her there is a mistake.

When Lewis Simpson, Robert Penn Warren, and others claimed Roberts for the Southern Renaissance, they wrote her into a tradition and provided a set of questions and answers for her work. For Simpson, the question her work asks is: "What does it mean to be a writer of the American South in the modern world?"; and he sees in her "an eminently self-conscious participant in [an] act of thought" that envisioned "Kentucky as the result of the modern mind's transference of a wilderness into itself," her project "the big myth of history" (*Fable* xiv, 57).

Simpson exemplifies what David M. Jordan has called "modernist regionalism," a regionalism that "conflates regional borders with epistemological borders" and leads the modernist regionalist to portray the region "as an autonomous world whose borders are under constant threat from external forces" (54). (I would not say, incidentally, that Rubin and others who institutionalized southern literary study at midcentury identified with this form of "modernist regionalism," or at least they did not do so consistently.)

Others have written Roberts into other traditions. Early on, Louis Auchincloss read her as one of the women writers who wrote America. More recently, Jill LeRoy-Frazier reads her as an Appalachian writer, not a southern one, and finds efforts to place Roberts in a southern tradition wrongheaded. For LeRoy-Frazier, Roberts's work is most definitely not characterized by that "sense of tragic loss and nostalgia" that was such a predominant theme in the criticism of the southernists of Roberts's era (and somewhat beyond her era): Roberts's work, LeRoy-Frazier writes, "does not figure [. . .] demise [. . .] as a traumatic final end, leading to regret, ruin, and the desire to escape into the glory of the past. [. . .] Rather, it is the image of an end which is also the beginning of a next stage, merely one point in a continuing cycle (that is, simple 'change,')"—and, for LeRoy-Frazier, this is Appalachian, not southern. Because Roberts was not herself Appalachian, Le-Roy-Frazier reads this displacement of "tragic loss and nostalgia" by an acceptance of "change" in Roberts's work to be the result of "her life experiences with inhabitants of the more mountainous regions of Kentucky, where she taught in the rural schools" (64).

I'm not buying LeRoy-Frazier's argument, not entirely, although it is compelling. Yes, in Roberts the "end" is a beginning, "a beginning before the beginning," but there is no "merely" about it. Diony Hall Jarvis, Ellen Chesser, and Theodosia Bell have, in their characterizations, too much in the way of personal desire and hope for that submergence into the "continuing cycle" to be so reassuring. There is violence and loss there as well, something of a melancholy more akin to Poe than Jefferson. And as for her work simply being an engagement with nationalist history, that too seems reductive. There is an undercurrent of folk romance in her work that speaks less to historical dialectics or great designs than to cultural patterns that may be more ethnographic or anthropological.

As for Simpson's sense of her southernness, Roberts was an Upper South writer, living between the Upper South and the Midwest. She was not, after all, educated at Vanderbilt or the University of North Carolina at Chapel Hill but at the University of Chicago, matriculating in 1917, part of a post–World War I literary renaissance that was not the Southern Renaissance of Allen Tate and John Crowe Ransom but the Chicago renaissance of Edgar Lee Masters, Carl Sandburg, Vachel Lindsay, and Harriet Monroe. There may be more *Spoon River Anthology* and *Winesburg, Ohio* in her than *Barren Ground* or *The Sound and the Fury* or "Antique Harvesters," John Crowe Ransom's evocative poem about the South's relationship to history, a fact that underscores my argument that the mapping of regions and regionalisms needs to be more flexible, more fluid, in the work of literary history.

One of the reasons Roberts has not been read very well, and possibly among the reasons she is so seldom read at all at present, may be this practice of writing her into prefabricated categories that don't fit this "North of the South" in which four traditions (national, southern, midwestern, and Appalachian) are in play. Is she an "American" writer who belongs in a tradition of women, or is she a "southern" writer asking what it means to be a writer of the American South in the modern world? Is she an Appalachian writer who finds peace in the cycle of history or in time itself? Is she a midwestern writer whose affinities are with Sherwood Anderson and Vachel Lindsay in her rendition of a melancholy and somewhat grotesque folk spirit? Is she something else? Janet Galligani Casey argues that readers in the 1920s and 1930s, when Roberts was writing, were much more interested in the difference between the rural and the urban than in regionalist distinctions (95). Maybe we should think more in these terms and look for traditions of rural writing across and beyond the United States; maybe such an inquiry would add importantly to our understanding of region. So many roads . . .

Roberts is, to my mind, a writer whose work is defined by the road, but not by just any road. Her work is defined by the road that leads from the Chesapeake Bay Cultural Hearth, past the swamp, past Richmond, past Jefferson's Albemarle County, over Poe's Ragged Mountains and the Appalachian plateau, and into that Upper South that attracted migrants from Pennsylvania and other Mid-Atlantic states, and where, as Jack Greene puts it, a South emerged in a region that would be "as heterogeneous as any other area of the . . . United States" ("Early Modern" 537–38).

What all this comes to is that we need new and more fluid regionalisms, new ways to map regions. I'm not ready to abandon regionalisms altogether, because, like the "local," they are recognizable carriers for ideas of place and affiliation, and regionalisms are, for reasons that have to do with the structures and trajectories of human life at present, resurgent in American literature. Michael Kowalewski, whom I quoted in chapter 1, reminds us that mappings can "put places into motion, making them move within their own history, both human and nonhuman." That history includes regionalisms. Like the local, they can inscribe the anachronistic, the marginal remainder, the not fully interpellated, the something left over after the assimilationist project—but importantly, and like other discourses of place, they also carry the potential for inscribing something of the emergent: beginnings and beginnings "before the beginning," beginnings inseparable from endings.

On the topics of wilderness, history, memory, forgetting, melancholy origins, endings, and the emergent, I'd like to close with another beginning before the beginning. In 2008 Toni Morrison published *A Mercy*, another novel that takes up the subject of the origins of the United States in a melancholy tenor. It is a kind of prequel to familiar narratives of the

American Revolution as well as to her own corpus of historical novels, from *Song of Solomon* to *Paradise*—novels that inscribe a journey that begins in "the North of the South" (recall the Virginia setting of Milkman Dead's journey into his origins in *Song of Solomon*) and moves westward to Missouri in *Beloved*, north to Harlem and back to the South in *Jazz*, and west to Oklahoma in *Paradise*. In short, *A Mercy* is a springboard for the migrations that define Morrison's earlier work and an alternative look at the story of American origins.

The novel tells the story of contact and encounter, farming and trade, class and race, ambition, servitude, slavery, disease, and (importantly) failure in the British colonies of North America between 1682 and 1690, a century before the American Revolution. Jacob Vaark is an Anglo-Dutch settler with a farm and a knack for making money; he is also a trader. His wife, Rebekka, is a virtuous and hardworking mail-order bride from Europe with whom Jacob is pleased. Like her husband, Rebekka is unencumbered by the religious sensibilities of her neighbors, sensibilities that lead them to see devils and demons in difference. Lina is an American Indian, a young survivor whose village has been burned following the death of its people from smallpox, a disease of the Columbian Exchange that eventually takes Jacob's life and scars Rebekka both physically and spiritually. Sorrow is a ship captain's daughter of mixed blood, left traumatized as the result of being the only survivor of a shipwreck. Willard and Scully are indentured servants, tricked into long years of service beyond their original terms of indenture. Florens is a young enslaved girl traded to Jacob by a Maryland planter in exchange for a debt; the girl (about nine or ten years old at the beginning of the story) is pressed upon Vaark's attention by her mother, who hopes to save her early blooming daughter from the attentions of the white men on the plantation. She sees in Jacob a man who looks at Florens and sees "a human child" (166), not an object of exchange. It is a novel of multiple focalizations. And as readers have noted, all of these are voices marginalized or erased by the conventional story of the colonization of North America.

But it is Florens whose story is most central in this novel with several centers, both in terms of place and character. She, reminiscent of the title character in Morrison's 1987 novel *Beloved*, embodies devastation. She does not understand why her mother throws her away (which is how she interprets her mother's unspoken act of love), and when the free man whom she loves also pushes her away, telling her that she is "nothing but wilderness. No constraint. No mind" (141), her transfiguration into wilderness personified is complete.

The violence and terror of "wildness" and "wilderness" as human conditions are central to Morrison's work from its beginnings (recall the feathered wildness associated with the iron bit Paul D is forced to wear in *Beloved*), but in *A Mercy*, wildness—that terror, that dangerous extremity of the human condition—becomes foundational to the American project itself. Mina Karavanta identifies the central question Morrison asks in *A Mercy*: "What is there before the time of the nation, at the very beginnings of transatlantic modernity?" (724).

What is there is a natural world. The geography of *A Mercy* has been much discussed—is it set in Maryland and Virginia (as La Vinia Delois Jennings has suggested), or is the Vaark farm in upstate New York or Massachusetts (as Susan Neal Mayberry and others have argued)? It must be force of habit, and possibly the fact that part of the novel is indeed set in Maryland and Virginia, that led Sandra Gustafson and Gordon Hutner, in a 2010 issue of *American Literary History*, to reference the "close ties" this novel suggests "between Southern slaveholding societies and the West Indies" (247).

Jacob's journey does begin in the Chesapeake Bay area—the world Poe would know 150 years later. Maryland's Catholicism is central to the story, and the main crop of the Maryland plantation is tobacco. Willard and Scully hail from a climate warmer than Jacob's farm. But, as one reader observes, *A Mercy* is also a primer on New England history—

King Philip's War, the witchcraft trials, and so on (Logan 194). It seems clear the Vaark farm is in upstate New York or Massachusetts (as attested to by the weather, the surrounding towns, the Anabaptists). Jacob's tragedy, as well as the ruination of his farm's inhabitants, happens just as his new mansion (a plantation structure), inspired by a late-arriving dream of wealth and status funded by investments in Barbadian sugar and rum—and fundamentally at odds with his earlier values—begins to take form. In short, Jacob Vaark's plantation dreams take shape well north of the South.

Morrison is historically accurate. Despite the continued belief (among academics as well as the general public) that slaveholding in the northern colonies was limited in scope to small holdings of a few enslaved persons in a household, excavations in Massachusetts, New York, and New Jersey beginning in the late 1990s attest to the existence there, between the early seventeenth century and the early nineteenth century, of large plantations dependent on enslaved labor. A thirteen-thousand-acre plantation owned by Samuel Browne has been excavated outside of Salem, Massachusetts, and there is evidence that more than one hundred enslaved people lived there over a period of sixty years in the eighteenth century. And on Long Island, an eight-thousand-acre plantation has been excavated on the site of Sylvester Manor. Both of these plantations had strong ties to Barbados and to the importation of sugar and rum (not to mention human beings to be exchanged as commodities) from that British possession, and to Dutch traders like Morrison's fictional Jacob Vaark.[1]

I have no doubt whatsoever that Morrison was aware of this history. Aside from the fact that she taught for years at Princeton, which has historical ties to slavery and was exploring those ties during the first decade of the twenty-first century when she was writing the book, her work is based in a deep historical sensibility that challenges the foundational complacencies of nationalist literary history—among them the idea that slavery and its legacies are regional aberrations rather than foundational to national wealth and nationalist ideology.

The fact is that there is no direct reference at all, anywhere in this novel, to a North/South divide. It is a prenational, preregional geography that Morrison references. Not even the Maryland planter is a southerner—he is Portuguese by way of Angola. In short, the novel is built from journeys that cross the stipulated boundary between North and South (a boundary not to be mapped for close to eighty years after the end of the novel) and, in the process, cross other boundaries—of race, class, nation. *A Mercy*'s world, like Poe's, Roberts's, and our own, is a crossroads.

Ultimately, *A Mercy* is a story of orphans black and white, people "thrown away" (as Morrison puts it) for one reason or another onto the shores of the New World, who find each other and, for a moment (less than a decade), deal more or less humanely with each other within the confines of Jacob Vaark's farm. The novel tells of the provisional alliances they create and the ultimate failure of those alliances.

At the end of the novel, autumn has come, and Florens, having been rejected by the man she loves, has never before seen "leaves make this much blood and brass," with "[c]olor so loud it hurts the eye" (158). It is from an emotional place of rage and devastation that she haunts the new mansion that Vaark has built with his profits from rum ("blood and brass" of a different sort), writing on its walls in hopes that "the telling" will enable her to cry, to mourn, but to no avail (158). Maybe fire, she thinks, "the air that is out in the world" (161), will make her story legible; maybe her words "[n]eed to fly up then fall, fall like ash over acres of primrose and mallow. Over a turquoise lake, beyond the eternal hemlocks, through clouds cut by rainbow and flavor the soil of the earth" (161).

Scully reflects: "They once thought they were a kind of family because together they had carved companionship out of isolation. But the family they imagined they had become was false. Whatever each one loved, sought or escaped, their futures were separate and anyone's guess. [. . .] Minus bloodlines, he saw nothing yet on the horizon to unite them" (155–56). Like Diony in Roberts's *The Great Meadow*, Scully knows that he and his compatriots on the Vaark farm were, as Roberts puts it, "a beginning before the beginning."

Florens's rage and Scully's summation are as applicable to our own postnational era—with its resurgent hate, its tribal loyalties—as to the prenational era from which Morrison has her characters speak. This is one source of the novel's power, and one of the reasons I wanted to end with *A Mercy*, because it looks back from the present to reimagine the story of our national origins and—in spite of (or perhaps because of) its traumatic narrative of loss—hold out a promise for the future in ways that, from the perspective of today, seem much more viable than many of the stories with which we are most familiar. Among those ways is the prospect of something, some thread of belief or value or shared experience, that might unite us in the face of difference.

Notes

≈

Introduction

1. To my disappointment, I learned that the title of my book, *The North of the South*, which I thought I had made up, was first used (to my knowledge) by Lois Leveen in a blog post for the *New York Times* in January 2011. "Richmond," she writes, "was . . . different from most other slave cities. It was the north of the South, with a more diverse population and economy than all but a handful of other Southern cities. . . . [It was] an industrialized urban center with strong economic ties to the North and West as well as the South" and "home to slaveowners and slaves, white immigrants and free blacks. . . . It was a microcosm of the Upper South on the eve of the Civil War." In this book and in the lectures it is based on, "North of the South" is somewhat larger, referring to South Carolina north of Sullivan's Island, North Carolina, Virginia, Delaware, Maryland, West Virginia, Kentucky, and Tennessee.

Chapter 1. Southern Literary Studies

1. For other valuable discussions of place, see Cheney, Dainotto, Harvey, and Pred.

2. Dealing primarily with Richmond in the 1850s, Kimball's book *American City, Southern Place* provides a detailed picture of life in the "American" city and its connections with the "southern" countryside and with slavery. He notes that Virginia was "the only Southern state that truly developed a system of cities" and that "Virginia's urban population increased 63.3 percent" between 1840 and 1860, while the state's rural population grew only 19 percent (39).

Chapter 2. Edgar Allan Poe

1. Robert Lawson-Peebles makes a fascinating suggestion that, to my knowledge, has not been picked up by later scholars. He finds, in the "looming" of this figure at the end of *Pym*, a possible trace of Henry James Pye's "The Progress of Refinement," a poem first published in 1783 in which Pye writes that "in the sad extremes of polar frost, / [. . .] / Man scarcely rises from the shaggy brood / That prowl insatiate o'er the icy flood" — and even more compellingly, a trace of *Hermsprong*, a novel by Robert Bage that appeared in the United States in 1803. Hermsprong (the protagonist himself) tells of a legendary western territory at the center of which is a lake named the White Bear. This lake is the location of two warring species: that of bears and that of men. When the two sides meet for a parley, they witness the appearance, from the water, of a huge figure: "viewed from one side, it seemed to be a bear; on the other, it seemed to be a man. The white bear part of this awful figure waved its paw in the air to command silence, then said, with a terrific voice . . ." "The tale breaks off here," Lawson-Peebles writes, "to point the moral that, however incredible, the traditions of alternative cultures must be respected" (275).

2. Poe's mention of Chapman's dark landscapes and the Dismal Swamp in "Philosophy of Furniture" is yet another subtle allusion to the Jeffersonian vision. See Anna O. Marley's explorations of the significance of Jefferson's many paintings of westward vistas at Monticello in her "Landscapes of the New Republic at Thomas Jefferson's Monticello."

3. Only a few have examined the Native American presence in Poe. Among them are J. Gerald Kennedy, in "'A Mania for Composition'"; Leon Jackson, in "'Behold Our Literary Mohawk, Poe'"; Maria Karafilis, in "American Racial Dystopia"; and Michael J. S. Williams, in "Poe's Ugly American."

Chapter 3. Backwater

1. For further reading on this subject, see Katherine Howlett Hayes's *Slavery before Race: Europeans, Africans, and Indians at Long Island's Sylvester Manor Plantation, 1651–1884* and Mac Griswold's *The Manor: Three Centuries at a Slave Plantation on Long Island.*

Bibliography

Armitage, David, and Michael J. Braddick, eds. *The British Atlantic World, 1500–1800.* New York: Palgrave Macmillan, 2002.

Auchincloss, Louis. *Pioneers and Caretakers: A Study of Nine American Women Novelists.* Minneapolis: University of Minnesota Press, 1965.

Augustine. From *Confessions.* Translated by R. S. Pine-Coffin. In *The Anatomy of Memory: An Anthology,* edited by James McConkey, 5–8. New York: Oxford University Press, 1996.

Benjamin, Walter. "Theses on the Philosophy of History." In *Illuminations: Essays and Reflections,* translated by Harry Zohn, edited by Hannah Arendt, 253–64. New York: Schocken Books, 1985.

Bondurant, Agnes M. *Poe's Richmond.* Richmond: Garrett & Massie, 1942.

Campbell, Harry Modean, and Ruel E. Foster. *Elizabeth Madox Roberts: American Novelist.* Norman: University of Oklahoma Press, 1956.

Campbell, SueEllen, Alex Hunt, Richard Kerridge, Tom Lynch, and Ellen Wohl. *The Face of the Earth: Natural Landscapes, Science, and Culture.* Berkeley: University of California Press, 2011. https://www.jstor.org/stable/10.1525/j.ctt1pn6d6.4.

Carter, Boyd. "Poe's Debt to Charles Brockden Brown." *Prairie Schooner* 27, no. 2 (Summer 1953): 190–96.

Casey, Edward S. *The Fate of Place: A Philosophical History.* Berkeley: University of California Press, 1997.

Casey, Janet Galligani. *A New Heartland: Women, Modernity, and the Agrarian Ideal in America.* New York: Oxford University Press, 2009.

Cecil, L. Moffitt. "Poe's Tsalal and the Virginia Springs." *Nineteenth-Century Fiction* 19, no. 4 (March 1965): 398–402.

Cheney, Jim. "Postmodern Environmental Ethics: Ethics as Bioregional Narrative." *Environmental Ethics: An Interdisciplinary Journal Dedicated to the Philosophical Aspects of Environmental Problems* 11, no. 2 (Summer 1989): 117–34.

Clukey, Amy, and Jeremy Wells. "Introduction: Plantation Modernity." *The Global South* 10, no. 2 (Fall 2016): 1–10.

Dainotto, Roberto Maria. "'All the Regions Do Smilingly Revolt': The Literature of Place and Region." *Critical Inquiry* 22, no. 3 (Spring 1996): 486–505.

Dayan, Joan. "Amorous Bondage: Poe, Ladies, and Slaves." *American Literature* 66, no. 2 (June 1994): 239–73.

Deleuze, Gilles, and Félix Guattari. *Anti-Oedipus: Capitalism and Schizophrenia.* Translated by Robert Hurley, Mark Seem, and Helen R. Lane. Minneapolis: University of Minnesota Press, 1983.

Duck, Leigh Anne. *The Nation's Region: Southern Modernism, Segregation, and U.S. Nationalism.* Athens: University of Georgia Press, 2006.

Eliot, T. S. "From Poe to Valéry." *The Hudson Review* 2, no. 3 (Autumn 1949): 327–42.

Evernden, Neil. "Beyond Ecology: Self, Place, & the Pathetic Fallacy." *North American Review* 263, no. 4 (Winter 1978): 16–20.

Fox-Genovese, Elizabeth. *Within the Plantation Household: Black and White Women of the Old South.* Chapel Hill: University of North Carolina Press, 1988.

Genovese, Eugene. *The World the Slaveholders Made: Two Essays in Interpretation.* New York: Pantheon Books, 1969.

Gough, Robert J. "The Myth of the 'Middle Colonies': An Analysis of Regionalization in Early America." *The Pennsylvania Magazine of History and Biography* 107, no. 3 (July 1983): 393–419.

Greene, Jack P. "Colonial South Carolina and the Caribbean Connection." *South Carolina Historical Magazine* 88, no. 4 (1987): 192–210.

Greene, Jack P. "Early Modern Southeastern North America and the Broader Atlantic and American Worlds." *The Journal of Southern History* 73, no. 3 (August 2007): 525–38.

Greene, Jack P., and J. R. Pole. "Reconstructing British-American Colonial History: An Introduction." In *Colonial British America: Essays in the New History of the Early Modern Era,* edited by Jack P. Greene and J. R. Pole. Baltimore: Johns Hopkins University Press, 1984.

Greeson, Jennifer Rae. *Our South: Geographic Fantasy and the Rise of National Literature*. Cambridge: Harvard University Press, 2010.

Griswold, Mac. *The Manor: Three Centuries at a Slave Plantation on Long Island*. New York: Farrar, Straus and Giroux, 2013.

Gustafson, Sandra M., and Gordon Hutner. "Projecting Early American Literary Studies." *American Literary History* 22, no. 2 (Summer 2010): 245–49.

Hall, Basil. *Travels in North America in the Years 1827 and 1828*. Vol. 3. Edinburgh: Cadell, 1829. HathiTrust Digital Library.

Harvey, David. *Justice, Nature, and the Geography of Difference*. Malden, Mass.: Blackwell, 1996.

Hayes, Katherine Howlett. *Slavery before Race: Europeans, Africans, and Indians at Long Island's Sylvester Manor Plantation, 1651–1884*. New York: New York University Press, 2013.

Holman, C. Hugh. *Three Modes of Modern Southern Fiction: Ellen Glasgow, William Faulkner, Thomas Wolfe*. Mercer University Lamar Memorial Lectures, no. 9. Athens: University of Georgia Press, 1966.

Hubbell, Jay B. "Poe and the Southern Literary Tradition." *Texas Studies in Literature and Language* 2, no. 2 (Summer 1980): 151–71.

Hutchison, Coleman. "The Brand New Southern Studies Waltz." Forum: What's New in Southern Studies—And Why Should We Care?, edited by Brian Ward. *Journal of American Studies* 48, no. 3 (August 2014): 694–97.

Jackson, Leon. "'Behold Our Literary Mohawk, Poe': Literary Nationalism and the 'Indianation' of Antebellum American Culture." *ESQ* 48 (2002): 97–133.

Jefferson, Thomas. *Notes on the State of Virginia*. 1785. Edited with an introduction and notes by Frank Shuffelton. New York: Penguin Books, 1999.

Jennings, La Vinia Delois. "*A Mercy*: Toni Morrison Plots the Formation of Racial Slavery in Seventeenth-Century America." *Callaloo* 32, no. 2 (Spring 2009): 645–49.

Jones, Anne Goodwyn. *Tomorrow Is Another Day: The Woman Writer in the South, 1859–1936*. Baton Rouge: Louisiana State University Press, 1981.

Jordan, David M. *New World Regionalism: Literature in the Americas*. Toronto: University of Toronto Press, 1994.

Karafilis, Maria. "American Racial Dystopia: Expansion and Extinction in Poe and Hawthorne." *Poe Studies* 48 (2015): 17–33.

Karavanta, Mina. "Toni Morrison's *A Mercy* and the Counterwriting of Negative Communities: A Postnational Novel." *MFS Modern Fiction Studies* 58, no. 4 (Winter 2012): 723–46.

Kennedy, J. Gerald. "'A Mania for Composition': Poe's Annus Mirabilis and the Violence of Nation-Building." *American Literary History* 17, no. 1 (2005): 1–35.

Kimball, Gregg D. *American City, Southern Place: A Cultural History of Antebellum Richmond*. Athens: University of Georgia Press, 2003.

Kowalewski, Michael. "Writing in Place: The New American Regionalism." *American Literary History* 6, no. 1 (Spring 1994): 171–83.

Ladd, Barbara. "Local Places/Modern Spaces: The Crossroads Local in Faulkner." In *Faulkner's Geographies: Faulkner and Yoknapatawpha 2011*, edited by Jay Watson and Ann J. Abadie, 3–16. Jackson: University Press of Mississippi, 2015.

Lawson-Peebles, Robert. *Landscape and Written Expression in Revolutionary America: The World Turned Upside Down*. Cambridge Studies in American Literature and Culture. Cambridge: Cambridge University Press, 1988.

LeRoy-Frazier, Jill. "'. . . full of decay which was change, not evil': Southern Literature, (Oral) History, and the Mountain South." *Southern Studies: An Interdisciplinary Journal of the South*, n.s., 7, no. 2 (1996): 57–77.

Lesquereux, Léo. *Lettres Écrites d'Amérique*. Neuchâtel: Imprimerie de Henri Wolfrath, 1853.

Leveen, Lois. "The North of the South." *Opinionator* (blog). *New York Times*, January 24, 2011. https://opinionator.blogs.nytimes.com/2011/01/24/the-north-of-the-south.

Levin, Harry. *The Power of Blackness: Hawthorne, Poe, Melville*. New York: Alfred A. Knopf, 1967.

Logan, Lisa M. "Thinking with Toni Morrison's *A Mercy* (A Response to 'Remembering the Past: Toni Morrison's Seventeenth Century in Today's Classroom')." *Early American Literature* 48, no. 1 (2013): 193–99.

Marley, Anna O. "Landscapes of the New Republic at Thomas Jefferson's Monticello." In *Building the British Atlantic World: Spaces, Places, and Material Culture, 1600–1850*, edited by Daniel Maudlin and Bernard L. Herman, 78–99. Chapel Hill: University of North Carolina Press, 2016.

Mattison, Lewis. "Life of the Town." In *Richmond, Capital of Virginia; Approaches to Its History, by Various Hands*. Advisory editor, H. J. Eckenrode. N.p.: Whittet & Shepperson, 1938.

Mayberry, Susan Neal. Review of *Toni Morrison's "A Mercy": Critical Approaches*, edited by Shirley A. Stave and Justine Tally. *African American Review* 45, no. 3 (Fall 2012): 463–66.

McCarthy, Cormac. *Child of God*. New York: Random House, 1973.

McLuhan, Herbert Marshall. "Edgar Poe's Tradition." *The Sewanee Review* 52, no. 1 (Winter 1944): 24–33.

McNeil, Adam. "Black Rights and Black Citizenship in Antebellum Baltimore." Review of *Birthright Citizens: A History of Race and Rights in Antebellum America*, by Martha S. Jones. *Black Perspectives* (blog). African American Intellectual History Society, October 2, 2018. https://www.aaihs.org/black-rights-and-black-citizenship-in-antebellum-baltimore/.

Morgan, Robert. "Backwater." *The Southern Review* 41, no. 1 (Winter 2005): 1.

Morrison, Toni. *Beloved*. New York: Alfred A. Knopf, 1987.

Morrison, Toni. *A Mercy*. New York: Alfred A. Knopf, 2008.

Morrison, Toni. *Playing in the Dark: Whiteness and the Literary Imagination*. William C. Massey Jr. Lectures in American Studies. Cambridge: Harvard University Press, 1992.

Morrison, Toni. *Song of Solomon*. New York: Alfred A. Knopf, 1977.

Mumford, Lewis. *Sticks and Stones: A Study of American Architecture and Civilization*. New York: Boni and Liveright, 1924.

Murphy, John J. "Elizabeth Madox Roberts and the Civilizing Consciousness." *The Register of the Kentucky Historical Society* 64, no. 2 (April 1966): 110–20.

Norfolk Herald (extra), September 4, 1821. In *Early American Hurricanes, 1492–1870*, by David M. Ludlum, 83. The History of American Weather, no. 1. Boston: American Meteorological Society, 1963.

O'Brien, Michael. "A Heterodox Note on the Southern Renaissance." In *Rethinking the South: Essays in Intellectual History*, 157–78. Baltimore: Johns Hopkins University Press, 1988.

Percival, Thomas. *Speculations on the Perceptive Power of Vegetables: Addressed to the Literary and Philosophical Society of Manchester. By Thomas Percival, M. D. F. R. S. & S. A. &c.* Warrington, U.K.: Printed by W. Eyres, [1785]. Eighteenth Century Collections Online. Accessed July 18, 2021. https://link.gale.com/apps/doc/CW0107996469/ECCO?u=emory&sid=bookmark-ECCO&xid=cd0222bc&pg=1.

Philippon, Daniel J. "Poe in the Ragged Mountains: Environmental History and Romantic Aesthetics." *The Southern Literary Journal* 30, no. 2 (Spring 1998): 1–16.

Poe, Edgar Allan. "The Colloquy of Monos and Una." In *Collected Works of Edgar Allan Poe.* Vol. 2, *Tales and Sketches, 1831–1842*, edited by Thomas Ollive Mabbott, 608–17. Cambridge: Belknap Press of Harvard University Press, 1978.

Poe, Edgar Allan. Edgar Allan Poe to George Washington Poe, July 14, 1839. Edgar Allan Poe Society of Baltimore—Works—Letters, https://www.eapoe.org/works/letters/p3907140.htm.

Poe, Edgar Allan. "Fairyland." In *Collected Works of Edgar Allan Poe.* Vol. 1, *Poems*, edited by Thomas Ollive Mabbott, 140–41. Cambridge: Belknap Press of Harvard University Press, 1969.

Poe, Edgar Allan. "The Fall of the House of Usher." In *Collected Works of Edgar Allan Poe.* Vol. 2, *Tales and Sketches, 1831–1842*, edited by Thomas Ollive Mabbott, 397–417. Cambridge: Belknap Press of Harvard University Press, 1978.

Poe, Edgar Allan. "Introduction." In *Collected Works of Edgar Allan Poe.* Vol. 1, *Poems*, edited by Thomas Ollive Mabbott, 156–58. Cambridge: Belknap Press of Harvard University Press, 1969.

Poe, Edgar Allan. "The Lake—To—." In *Collected Works of Edgar Allan Poe.* Vol. 1, *Poems*, edited by Thomas Ollive Mabbott, 85–86. Cambridge: Belknap Press of Harvard University Press, 1969.

Poe, Edgar Allan. "Ligeia." In *Collected Works of Edgar Allan Poe.* Vol. 2, *Tales and Sketches, 1831–1842*, edited by Thomas Ollive Mabbott, 310–30. Cambridge: Belknap Press of Harvard University Press, 1978.

Poe, Edgar Allan. "Mesmeric Revelation." In *Collected Works of Edgar Allan Poe*. Vol. 3, *Tales and Sketches, 1843–1849*, edited by Thomas Ollive Mabbott, 1029–40. Cambridge: Belknap Press of Harvard University Press, 1978.

Poe, Edgar Allan. "The Name of the Nation." In *The Portable Edgar Allan Poe*, edited by J. Gerald Kennedy, 600. New York: Penguin Classics, 2006.

Poe, Edgar Allan. *The Narrative of Arthur Gordon Pym of Nantucket*. New York: Harper and Brothers, 1838. HathiTrust Digital Library. https://babel.hathitrust.org/cgi/pt?id=uc2.ark:/13960/t3xs5jt25&view=1up&seq=9&skin=2021.

Poe, Edgar Allan. "Philosophy of Furniture." In *Collected Works of Edgar Allan Poe*. Vol 2, *Tales and Sketches, 1831–1842*, edited by Thomas Ollive Mabbott, 495–503. Cambridge: Belknap Press of Harvard University Press, 1978.

Poe, Edgar Allan. "Silence—A Fable." In *Collected Works of Edgar Allan Poe*. Vol. 2, *Tales and Sketches, 1831–1842*, edited by Thomas Ollive Mabbott, 195–99. Cambridge: Belknap Press of Harvard University Press, 1978.

Poe, Edgar Allan. "A Tale of the Ragged Mountains." In *Collected Works of Edgar Allan Poe*. Vol. 3, *Tales and Sketches, 1843–1849*, edited by Thomas Ollive Mabbott, 939–50. Cambridge: Belknap Press of Harvard University Press, 1978.

Pollin, Burton R. "Edgar Allan Poe and John G. Chapman: Their Treatment of the Dismal Swamp and the Wissahickon." *Studies in the American Renaissance* (1983): 245–74.

Pred, Allan. "Place as Historically Contingent Process: Structuration and the Time-Geography of Becoming Places." *Annals of the Association of American Geographers* 74, no. 2 (June 1984): 279–97.

Renan, Ernest. "What Is a Nation?" Translated by E. J. Leonard. In *Cyclopaedia of Political Science, Political Economy, and of the Political History of the United States*. Vol 2, edited by John J. Lalor, 925. Chicago: M. B. Cary, 1883.

Roberts, David D. *Benedetto Croce and the Uses of Historicism*. Berkeley: University of California Press, 1987.

Roberts, Elizabeth Madox. *The Great Meadow*. New York: Viking Press, 1930.

Roberts, Elizabeth Madox. *My Heart and My Flesh*. New York: Viking Press, 1927.

Roberts, Elizabeth Madox. *The Time of Man.* New York: Viking Press, 1926.

Romine, Scott. *The Real South: Southern Narrative in the Age of Cultural Reproduction.* Baton Rouge: Louisiana State University Press, 2008.

Romine, Scott, and Jennifer Rae Greeson, eds. *Keywords for Southern Studies.* New Southern Studies Series. Athens: University of Georgia Press, 2016.

Rubin, Louis D., Jr. *The Edge of the Swamp: A Study in the Literature and Society of the Old South.* Baton Rouge: Louisiana State University Press, 1989.

Rubin, Louis D., Jr. "Southern Literature: A Piedmont Art." *The Mississippi Quarterly* 23, no. 1 (Winter 1969/70): 1–16.

Rubin, Louis D., Jr. "Thomas Wolfe and the Place He Came From." *VQR: A National Journal of Literature and Discussion* 52, no. 2 (Spring 1976). https://www.vqronline.org/essay/thomas-wolfe-and-place-he-came.

Sawyer, Roy T. *America's Wetland: An Environmental and Cultural History of Tidewater Virginia and North Carolina.* Charlottesville: University of Virginia Press, 2010.

Sayers, Daniel O. *A Desolate Place for a Defiant People: The Archaeology of Maroons, Indigenous Americans, and Enslaved Laborers in the Great Dismal Swamp.* Gainesville: University Press of Florida, 2014.

Shepard, Paul, and Daniel McKinley, eds. *The Subversive Science: Essays toward an Ecology of Man.* Boston: Houghton Mifflin, 1969.

Simpson, Lewis P. *The Fable of the Southern Writer.* Baton Rouge: Louisiana State University Press, 1994.

Simpson, Lewis P. "The Southern Recovery of Memory and History." *The Sewanee Review* 82, no. 1 (Winter 1974): 1–32.

Smyth, John F. D. "Narrative of John F. D. Smyth: 1769–1775." In *Travels in Virginia in Revolutionary Times*, edited by Alfred J. Morrison. Lynchburg, Va.: J. P. Bell, 1922.

Thomas, Dwight, and David K. Jackson. *The Poe Log: A Documentary Life of Edgar Allan Poe, 1809–1849.* Boston: G. K. Hall, 1987.

Williams, Michael J. S. "Poe's Ugly American: 'A Tale of the Ragged Mountains.'" *Poe Studies/Dark Romanticism* 32, no. 1/2 (1999): 51–61.

Williams, William Carlos. *In the American Grain*. New York: Albert & Charles Boni, 1925.

Wilson, Charles Reagan. "Place, Sense of." In *The New Encyclopedia of Southern Culture*. Vol. 4, *Myth, Manners, and Memory*, edited by Charles Reagan Wilson, 253–55. Chapel Hill: University of North Carolina Press, 2006.

Wood, Gillen D'Arcy. *Tambora: The Eruption That Changed the World*. Princeton: Princeton University Press, 2014. https://www.jstor.org/stable/j.ctt5vjv5c.11.

Index

꿈

Selected books from the Mercer University Lamar Memorial Lectures

Printed in the United States
by Baker & Taylor Publisher Services